RUN

THE LIFELONG PURSUITS OF A GODLY MAN

Tim Challies

@CHALLIES

AUTHOR

Tim Challies is a Christian, a husband to Aileen, and a father of three. He is a co-founder of Cruciform Press, and has written several books. He worships and serves as a pastor at Grace Fellowship Church in Toronto, Ontario and writes daily at http://www.challies.com.

TABLE OF CONTENTS

CruciformPress

We like to keep it simple. So we publish clear, useful, inexpensive books for Christians and other curious people. Books that make sense and are easy to read, even as they tackle serious subjects. We offer Christian life, Bible study, fiction titles, and more.

We do this because the good news of Jesus Christ—the gospel—is the only thing that actually explains why this world is so wonderful and so awful all at the same time. Even better, the gospel applies to every single area of life, and offers real answers that aren't available from any other source.

These are books you can afford, enjoy, finish easily, benefit from, and remember. Check us out and see.

CruciformPress.com

Run to Win: The Lifelong Pursuits of a Godly Man

Print / PDF ISBN: 978-1-941114-88-9
ePub ISBN: 978-1-941114-90-2
Mobipocket ISBN: 978-1-941114-89-6

THE RACE
WE RUN

Every four years the Summer Olympics begin again, and the whole world becomes obsessed with activities they haven't thought about since the previous Games. Suddenly we find ourselves waking up early and staying up late to watch athletes pole vault and throw javelins and dive into pools. We can't help but cheer as we watch little-known sports like field hockey and handball and water polo. What is it that compels us to watch these strange events and to cheer for people we don't even know?

We watch the Olympics because we want to see the best of the best. Athletes do not get to the Olympics simply because of natural talent or wishing upon a star. They do not earn the opportunity to represent their countries through parental privilege or dumb luck. They get to the Olympics by hard work, by committing their whole lives to the pursuit of their sport. They have bodies very much like ours—the same 650 muscles, the same 206 bones, the same two feet—yet they can do things that we can only dream of. We may not know much about high jump, but we do know that we are watching something that required thousands of hours of training. We may not know a tuck from a handspring, but we do know that it took years of painful labor to perform such an acrobatic move. They have become the best in the world because of their total devotion to their sport, because of their grueling training, and because of their rigid self-discipline.

THE RACE

In his first letter to the Corinthian church, the Apostle Paul uses athletes as a metaphor to describe how believers are to approach the Christian life: "Do you not know that in a race all the runners run, but only one receives the prize? So run that you may obtain it" (1 Corinthians 9:24).

Of course the Corinthians knew! Their city was the home of the Isthmian Games. Every two years, the best world's athletes would arrive, their minds set on claiming the prize. In that day, there were no team sports, so each athlete competed alone, and there were no consolation prizes, so each athlete competed to be first. Paul tells these believers to think of the Christian life as a race and to imitate the kind of athlete who runs not just to compete but to be victorious. Striving against the deadly competition of the world, the flesh, and the devil, he urges them, "Run in such a way that you may win" (NASB)!

But how? What must they do to ensure that they win this race? Paul continues: "Every athlete exercises self-control in all things" (1 Corinthians 9:25). Athletes become successful through self-control. They commit themselves wholeheartedly to their sport and put aside any vices, habits, or activities that might keep them from peak performance. The athletes who competed in the Isthmian Games underwent ten months of dedicated training. During that time, they followed a strict regimen of diet and exercise. They were absolutely single-minded in their pursuit of victory.

Paul is saying that just as self-control is essential to victory in athletics, it is essential to victory in the Christian life. Good intentions will not carry Christians to victory, half-hearted effort will bring no reward, lack of discipline will lead only to disqualification. By self-control athletes get the prize, and by self-control Christians get their reward.

So what was the reward these athletes stood to gain? "They do it to receive a perishable wreath, but we an imperishable" (1 Corinthians 9:25). In the early days of the Games, athletes were rewarded with a crown woven of dry celery leaves. Later, in Roman times, this was replaced by a wreath of pine. These crowns were organic and perishable, so in ten or twenty years they would fade to dust. Paul draws a comparison: if athletes exercise rigid discipline for the sake of a disintegrating wreath, shouldn't Christians labor even harder for a reward that will endure forever? Paul doesn't say what this reward is, but his point is clear: the Christian who wins this race receives a prize of immeasurable value and eternal duration.

Then Paul provides an illustration from his own disciplined life: "So I do not run aimlessly; I do not box as one beating the air. But I discipline my body and keep it under control, lest after preaching to others I myself should be disqualified" (1 Corinthians 9:26–27). Paul refuses to be like a half-hearted athlete, content to take a leisurely jog. He will not be like a boxer who shirks his training and ends up futilely flailing his fists in the air. Instead, he will be like a runner who is driven to vanquish the competition and like a fighter who has been trained to deliver brutal blows. He applies self-discipline to every part of his life—his body, mind, and soul. He exercises self-control to avoid sin and to practice godliness, to flee immorality and to pursue holiness. He allows nothing that increases the risk of disqualification. He is as committed to the Christian life as the greatest athlete is to his sport. He is determined to win his race, to receive his reward.

In Paul's mind, self-control brings freedom. Like an athlete, he exercises self-control to free himself to achieve what he most wants to achieve, to live how he truly wants to live. No longer controlled by illicit sexual desires, he can live in purity; no longer controlled by the love of money, he can be content with little; no longer controlled by the opinions of men, he can be satisfied in living for the glory of God. Self-control is the training regimen that will bring him to victory, the program that later allows him to proclaim this benediction upon his life: "I have fought the good fight, I have finished the race, I have kept the faith. Henceforth there is laid up for me the crown of righteousness, which the Lord, the righteous judge, will award to me on that day" (2 Timothy. 4:7–8).

RUN TO WIN!

I have written this book primarily for men who are running this race. Women can read it, too, and will benefit from it, I'm sure. (First Corinthians is an epistle that applies to men and women alike!) But I am writing specifically as a brother to my brothers. In this book, I will suggest a number of disciplines meant to help you compete at peak performance and assure you of victory. Each one will be an imperative, a command to consider and obey: Embrace your purpose! Renew your mind! Prioritize your church! Control your sexuality! Treasure your marriage! And many more. As I interact with men near and far, as I talk to the men I pastor, as I look within my own heart, I see far too much apathy and far too little zeal. I see men who are content to slumber instead of train. Men who treat life as if it's a leisurely jog instead of a grueling race. I see men who are unmotivated, who are uninspired by the imperishable reward that awaits across the finish line. I see men who are undisciplined, who regard self-control as a burden instead of a joy. I see men who are indifferent, who seem to care little whether they break the tape in victory or are shamefully disqualified. I want these men to know that the race is on! I want them to long for the prize, and I want them to begin or renew a lifelong regimen of self-control to obtain it.

My friend, you are in the race for the imperishable prize. Are you running to obtain it? You have no hope of victory unless you are determined to prevail and unless you prove your determination with dedication and discipline. Will you follow along as we explore how to run with zeal and self-control? You've got just one life to live, one race to run. So live it with all your might, and run to win!

STRENGTH FOR THE RACE

You can't run the race and win the prize in your own strength—you need God's help to do it. In the same chapter where Paul talks about disciplining himself like an athlete, he also says, "For if I preach the gospel, that gives me no ground for boasting" (1 Corinthians 9:16). He understood what Jesus meant when he said, "I am the vine; you are the branches. Whoever abides in me and I in him, he it is that bears much fruit, for apart from me you can do nothing" (John 15:5). As you continue reading this book, pray for strength from the Holy Spirit to practice the disciplines discussed, and look to the cross and resurrection of Jesus Christ for hope and help when you realize how far you have fallen short. Because he died and rose for us, full forgiveness and abundant new life is available to you at any moment, for this is what the Lord himself says to us:

> Come to me, all who labor and are heavy laden, and I will give you rest. Take my yoke upon you, and learn from me, for I am gentle and lowly in heart, and you will find rest for your souls. For my yoke is easy, and my burden is light. (Matthew 11:28–30)

PART 1

DISCIPLINES OF FAITH

EMBRACE YOUR PURPOSE

At this very moment, you are running a race. You are running a race even if you are sitting on the bus reading these words on your phone, or even if you are reading this to take a break from the drudgery of your work. Everywhere and at all times you are running the race of all races, the Christian life. The question is not *if* you are running but how. Are you running well or running poorly? Are you out for a leisurely jog, or are you sprinting hard with your eyes on the prize? Through the living Word, the Apostle Paul pleads with you, "Run to win! Run to win the prize!"

In this book, I am calling men away from apathy toward a zealous pursuit of the imperishable prize, away from worthless habits toward godly disciplines, away from aimless wandering toward purposeful living. This chapter will center on one imperative for winning this race. It is fitting that we begin with the matter of purpose, for only when you know your purpose will you be motivated to run this race and to run it with all the effort required to win it. Only then will you be able to share the joyful conviction of George Whitefield, who declared, "I am never better than when I am on the full stretch for God." My friend, if you are going to run to win, if you are going to be on the full stretch for God, you must embrace your purpose.

THE PURPOSE OF YOUR SALVATION

Why did God save you? Paul tells you exactly why:

> For the grace of God has appeared, bringing salvation for all people, training us to renounce ungodliness and worldly passions, and to live self-controlled, upright, and godly lives in the present age, waiting for our blessed hope, the appearing of the glory of our great God and Savior Jesus Christ, who gave himself for us to redeem us from all lawlessness and to purify for himself a people for his own possession who are zealous for good works. (Titus 2:11–14)

It would take whole volumes of books to unpack all that Paul says here, but I will make just a few observations.

First, God saves you to sanctify you. God extends his saving mercy to you so he can undo the deep damage caused by your sin. In a moment he redeems you, and over a lifetime he purifies you, teaching you to hate and renounce whatever is ungodly and to love and pursue whatever is worthy. As you walk with Christ, you find a new longing to put to death those old deeds and the desires that motivated them and to bring to life new deeds born of purer desires (Colossians 3:1–17). This is called *sanctification*, the lifelong process of becoming holy. God saves you to sanctify you, to restore you to the life he intended for you before you gave yourself to sin.

Second, God saves and sanctifies you so you can do good to others. Your sanctification has a purpose: to make you "zealous for good works" (Titus 2:14). Good works are deeds that are done not primarily for your own good but for the good of others. You are called to put aside the natural selfishness that once controlled you and to put on the Christ-like selflessness that compels you to bless to others. You are to live as a good-works extremist, a man who will stop at nothing to be a blessing to others. "We are [God's] workmanship," says Paul, "created in Christ Jesus *for good works,* which God prepared beforehand, that we should walk in them" (Ephesians 2:10).

Third, God does all things for his glory. God does not save you so he can make much of you, but so you can make much of him. The good deeds you do are not meant to make yourself look great but to make God look great. They stand as proof of the great change he has worked within you, for only by his grace can you turn your desires away from your own comfort, your own enrichment, your own fame. "Let your light shine before others," says Jesus, "so that they may see your good works and give glory to your Father who is in heaven" (Matthew 5:16).

Men, this is your purpose: to bring glory to God by doing good for others. This means your life is not first about you.

You are not the point of your existence or the hero of your salvation. You were created by God and for God. You were saved to bring glory to God by doing good to others. This is your purpose.

However, I suspect you already know most of this. The problem is that you still struggle to find enough motivation to bring to your life the focused self-control that will enable you to run to win. So let's turn back to Paul to see where he found the motivation to embrace this God-glorifying purpose.

EXTRAORDINARY FERVOR

An athlete runs to receive a reward and to enjoy the fame and acclaim that come with it. All the training, the exertion, and the self-control are judged to be worth it when the wreath is placed upon his head and when the crowd stands to pay tribute. His self-control is driven by the greatness of the prize. So what prize could be sufficient to motivate Paul to live this life of extraordinary fervor and intense zeal? Only one thing: Jesus Christ. Paul, once the self-proclaimed chief of sinners, had been suddenly and dramatically saved by Jesus. In a moment he had been plucked off the highway to hell and set upon the pathway to heaven. He was forever transformed. And with this new life, he had a new purpose. He now lived to be a faithful representative of Jesus Christ, to be absolutely devoted to growing in Christlikeness and making Jesus known to those around him. When Paul embraced Jesus Christ—or rather, when Jesus embraced Paul—Paul also embraced a new purpose.

Men, have you been transformed by Jesus Christ? Have you been given new life? With new life comes a new purpose! Let go of the ridiculous notion that your life is about you. Let go of all the selfish purposes you once held on to. Let go of the cultural wave of apathy and self-indulgence that is plaguing so many. And once you have let go of all that might hinder you, grab on to a lifelong pursuit of Jesus! Embrace your purpose and align every area of your life with it: you are here to glorify God by abounding in good works.

This is your challenge and mine. Your church needs you to be holy, to see a believer who has been set free from sin and who is committed to their good. Your neighborhood needs you to be holy, to see a man who has been utterly transformed by Jesus and who now puts aside anything that might hinder the gospel of Jesus. If you have a family, they need you to be holy, to see a husband and father who models what it means to be a mature Christian man. Your world needs you to be holy, to see evidence that Jesus Christ continues to save his people and continues to transform them into his image. In the inestimable prize of Jesus Christ, you have all the motivation you need to embrace a new purpose and fix your eyes on the glory of God.

DO IT NOW

Here are some practical ways that you can increase your motivation to live for the purpose of bringing glory to God:

- *Lay up treasure in heaven.* Jesus said,

  > Do not lay up for yourselves treasures on earth, where moth and rust destroy and where thieves break in and steal, but lay up for yourselves treasures in heaven, where neither moth nor rust destroys and where thieves do not break in and steal. For where your treasure is, there your heart will be also. (Matthew 6:19)

  The more time and energy you spend on spiritual endeavors (if done through the power of the Holy Spirit), the more your heart will become motivated to love and serve Christ. We place a high value on material possessions when we pay a lot of money for them or put a lot of time into them, and that "treasure principle" applies to our relationship with God as well.

- *Lift up the Lord in worship.* In Psalm 73 David describes how he was envying the prosperity of the wicked and thinking that his own pursuit of purity was in vain. But then he "went into the sanctuary of God" and was reminded that he would be much better off in the end (vv. 16–20). His God-centered, Word-centered worship caused him to value the Lord so much that he ended up saying, "Whom have I in heaven but you? And there is nothing on earth that I desire besides you" (v. 25).

- *Lead others to Christ.* In Luke 16 Jesus told a parable about an unjust steward who used his earthly treasure to build relationships with people who could help him in the future. Drawing a spiritual parallel, the Lord said, "Make friends for yourselves by means of unrighteous wealth, so that when it fails they may receive you into the eternal dwellings" (v. 9). The idea is that if you use your treasure, time, and talents for the sake of the kingdom in this life, you will be blessed with true friendships both now and in eternity. And this will make you more able to, in the words of the Westminster Shorter Catechism, "glorify God and enjoy him forever."

RUN TO WIN!

You are a few minutes farther into your race than you were when you began reading. You've taken a few more steps. And I hope you have come to see that if you are going to succeed in this race, you need to know the reason God saved and sanctifies you. Only then will you be motivated to put aside the selfishness of apathy and put on the selflessness of holiness. Embrace your purpose, then run to win!

Note: My book *Do More Better* is a practical guide to a life of productivity, with productivity defined as: "Effectively stewarding my gifts, talents, time, energy, and enthusiasm for the good of others and the glory of God." If this is an area of struggle for you, consider reading the book. (*See bit.ly/domorebetter*)

STRENGTH FOR THE RACE

In 2 Corinthians 5:14–15 Paul explains where he got his strength to run the race for God's glory: "The love of Christ controls us, because we have concluded this: that one has died for all, therefore all have died; and he died for all, that those who live might no longer live for themselves but for him who for their sake died and was raised." Jesus loved Paul even though he had been the foremost among sinners (1 Timothy 1:15) and Jesus died for us "while we were still sinners" (Romans 5:8). Knowing this keeps us from despair over our failures and gives us hope that through repentance and forgiveness we can bring glory to God in our lives regardless of how messed up they might be.

2

RENEW YOUR MIND

There are many places in the Bible where God presents a stark contrast between two options, then urges the reader to make a choice. He gave his law to ancient Israel, then said, "I have set before you life and death, blessing and curse. Therefore choose life" (Deuteronomy 30:19). In the Sermon on the Mount, Jesus contrasted wide and narrow gates and pleaded, "Enter by the narrow gate. For the gate is wide and the way is easy that leads to destruction, and those who enter by it are many. For the gate is narrow and the way is hard that leads to life, and those who find it are few" (Matthew 7:13–14).

Another of these contrasts is found at a key point in the book of Romans. For eleven chapters Paul has expounded on the gospel, describing what Christ has accomplished for Jews and Gentiles alike. Then he confronts his readers with a contrast and implies they must make a choice: "Do not be conformed to this world," he says, "but be transformed by the renewal of your mind" (12:2). There are only two options:

conformity or transformation. You can be conformed to this world or you can be transformed by the renewing of your mind. The choice lies before you every day.

Many of today's men have made a poor choice. They've chosen to conform, to feed their lust with the pornographic images of the world, to speak as the world speaks, to take on a sinful lifestyle marked by pride, apathy, and self-indulgence. If you are a Christian man, you are called to something different, something better, something far more challenging and far more satisfying. You are called to godliness. You are called to renounce anything that would hinder you in your race and to embrace a lifelong pursuit of knowing Jesus.

In this chapter we will consider how God calls men like you to live with the same discipline, dedication, and self-control that an Olympic athlete brings to the pursuit of the gold. Such commitment demands self-control that extends even to the mind. More accurately, it demands self-control that begins in the mind. To run to win, you must renew your mind.

A DARKENED MIND

At one point in your life, you were confronted with the choice of entering the wide gate or the narrow gate. If you are a Christian, that means you chose to enter the narrow gate and follow the way that leads to life. In that moment of decision, that moment of salvation, you experienced a kind of awakening. Your mind was suddenly able to understand that you are a sinner, that you had defied a holy God, and that Jesus Christ was offering reconciliation by grace through faith. The reason you had never before accepted this truth or embraced this Savior is that your mind had not been able to understand it. This truth was hidden from you because of your spiritual blindness.

Paul talks about this in his letter to the church in Ephesus:

Now this I say and testify in the Lord, that you must no longer walk as the Gentiles do, in the futility of their minds. They are darkened in their understanding, alienated from the life of God because of the ignorance that is in them, due to their hardness of heart. They have become callous and have given themselves up to sensuality, greedy to practice every kind of impurity. (Ephesians 4:17–19)

You were born in a state of sinfulness in which your futile mind could not understand the truth of the gospel.

The alarming fact is that sin not only made you *walk* in the darkness, it also darkened your understanding. Not only were you unable to do things that are pleasing to God, but you were also unable to even know what is pleasing to God (Romans 8:8, 1 Corinthians 2:14). But when you turned to Christ in repentance and faith, suddenly your mind was illumined by God so you could understand. You could understand who God is, who you are, and why the gospel is such good news. In a moment, your mind was given access to true and saving knowledge. In a moment you understood just how blind you had been for all those years. This is what Wesley celebrated in "And Can it Be," one of his greatest hymns: "Long my imprisoned spirit lay, fast bound in sin and nature's night; Thine eye diffused a quickening ray—I woke, the dungeon flamed with light. My chains fell off, my heart was free, I rose, went forth, and followed Thee."

You entered the Christian life with a mind that had just been pierced by that quickening ray of God's truth. But while your mind had been awakened, it was still far from perfected. Through the rest of life you are faced with the constant challenge, "Do not be conformed to this world, but be transformed by the renewal of your mind" (Romans 12:2). This choice is set before you each day: will you allow the world to conform your mind, or will you invite God to transform your mind? To not choose is to make a choice—the world is so immersive, so powerful, and so present that unless you actively resist it, you will inevitably be conformed to it and consumed by it.

DO NOT BE CONFORMED

When the Bible speaks of *the world*, it refers to any value system or way of life opposed to God and foreign to his Word. The world promotes "the desires of the flesh and the desires of the eyes and pride of life" (1 John 2:16). As a Christian man, God calls you to live on this earth surrounded by human society, yet to display a very different system of values and to exhibit a very different way of life. Even though you are a Christian, it is easy to be conformed to the world so that you begin to desire what the world desires, to think how the world thinks, and to behave like the world behaves.

Men are most often conformed to the world by carelessness, by neglecting to consider the allure of the world and by failing to guard against its encroachment. Just think of the countless seductive website advertisements that appeal to men who are ready to plunge into sinful desire. Think of the character traits displayed by men in popular sitcoms: ignorance, laziness, immaturity. Watch out for the unexpected gateways of conformity. It may be entertainment, when you fail to be cautious about what you watch, hear, and read, and when you fail to limit the time spent on entertainment. Sometimes the gateway is education, when you are influenced by people who are opposed to God. It may be friendships, when you maintain your most formative relationships with unbelievers. Or the main gateway of conformity may simply be neglect, when you fail to walk closely with God and instead allow the natural worldliness within your own heart to gain influence.

Worldliness is like gravity, always around you, always exerting its pressure. You must resist it because your spiritual life and health depend on it. You can resist it because you are indwelled by the Holy Spirit, who delights in transforming you by the renewing of your mind.

BE TRANSFORMED

For God to save you, he first had to open your mind to understand the truth of the gospel. But instead of immediately perfecting your mind, he assigned you the lifelong responsibility of renewing it. Just as a caterpillar undergoes the slow metamorphosis that transforms it into a butterfly, your mind is meant to undergo a steady, purposeful change as it is saturated and controlled by the Word of God. The Holy Spirit illumines the words of the Bible to your mind so you can understand and obey it. "We all, with unveiled face, beholding the glory of the Lord, are being transformed into the same image from one degree of glory to another. For this comes from the Lord who is the Spirit" (2 Corinthians 3:18). There are no shortcuts and no alternative paths. The one and only way your mind can be renewed is by the Spirit of God working through the Word of God.

Christian man, you must renew your mind. Which direction is your mind changing: toward conformity to the world or toward transformation into God's image? Which has more of an influence over your mind: the Sports page of the newspaper or the Word of God? Where do you find yourself more often: sitting on the couch watching television or bowing on your knees in prayer over the Word? Over a lifetime of commitment to God's Word, you gain new wisdom to replace old foolishness, and you gain godly desires to replace satanic longings. The sins that once fueled your imagination and motivated your actions begin to lose their power and are displaced by virtues that motivate good to others and bring glory to God. Your eyes stop their lusting because your mind is now filled with love; your mouth stops its cursing because your mind is now filled with joy; your hands stop their stealing because you are convinced you can be as content with little as with much. Such transformed lives begin with transformed minds, for your body always obeys your brain.

DO IT NOW

Here are some practical ways to help renew your mind:

- *Eliminate all temptations.* What causes your mind to
  think about the wrong things? Is it what you look at or
  listen to, places you go, or people you spend time with?
  When you know something is a stumbling block to you,
  take Jesus' advice in Matthew 5:29–30: "If your right eye
  causes you to sin, tear it out and throw it away…. And if
  your right hand causes you to sin, cut it off and throw it
  away. For it is better that you lose one of your members
  than that your whole body go into hell." This "principle
  of amputation" means that you should eliminate
  anything from your life that is preventing your mind
  from being renewed.

- *Replace the old with the new.* Ephesians 4:21–24 says you
  "were taught in him, as the truth is in Jesus, to put off your
  old self, which belongs to your former manner of life and
  is corrupt through deceitful desires, and to be renewed
  in the spirit of your minds, and to put on the new self,
  created after the likeness of God in true righteousness and
  holiness." It's not enough to just "put off" the bad influ-
  ences on your mind—you also have to "put on" or *replace*
  them with things that point you to Christ. Paul gives some
  practical examples in the verses following that passage,
  like replacing lying with speaking the truth and hurtful
  words with those that build up others. Make a list of sinful
  thoughts that you struggle with, and next to each write
  some true, biblical thoughts that you can "put on" instead.

RUN TO WIN!

Now the choice lies before you. Will you be conformed to this world or will you be transformed by the renewing of your mind? There is no mystery to either one. To be conformed to this world, you simply need to immerse yourself in it, to allow yourself to be influenced by it. It takes no effort and brings no true reward. To be transformed by the renewing of your mind, you need to immerse yourself in the Word of God, to allow yourself to be influenced by it. It takes great effort and brings great reward.

The Olympic runner longs to hear the crowd screaming his name and longs to feel the weight of the gold medal as it hangs around his neck. He determines in his mind that he must win and then instills habits that will force him to live with discipline, to train with persistence, and to put aside anything that might threaten his success. If he does all this for the adoration of mere men and the reward of a few ounces of metal, how much more should you, Christian, resolve to "lay aside every weight, and sin which clings so closely, and… run with endurance the race set before [you]" (Hebrews 12:1)? You run to hear your heavenly Father proclaim, "Well done, good and faithful servant" (Matthew 25:21) and to bestow on you a reward that can never fade and never be lost. If you are going to keep your legs moving toward the prize of Christ, you must keep your mind renewing toward the mind of Christ. Christian man, renew your mind!

STRENGTH FOR THE RACE

The command in Romans 12:2 to "be transformed by the renewing of your mind" is one of the ways "to present your bodies as a living sacrifice, holy and acceptable to God, which is your spiritual worship," as it says in the previous verse. And in that verse Paul highlights both our motivation and empowerment when he adds the phrase "by the mercies of God"—referring to all the blessings of God's grace that are discussed in the previous eleven chapters of Romans. That's why we should commit ourselves to renewing our minds, and how we can do it even though it runs counter to our sinful nature: God has graciously intervened to save us from the horrible consequences of sin (Romans 1–3); he has freely forgiven and justified us in Christ (Romans 4–5); he has given us the ability to live a new life by the power of the Holy Spirit (Romans 6–7); and he is working all things for good in our lives by his sovereign power and plan (Romans 8–11).

3

KNOW YOUR DOCTRINE

"Doctrine divides," the young man explained. "Of course it's important, but God cares far more for our deeds than our creeds. Doctrine divides, but love unites." Could he be right? Is doctrine a force for division, meant to bow before the primacy of love?

"I find doctrine boring," the husband confessed. "I don't have any interest in hearing about theology. Just tell me what God wants me to do, and I'll do it. I'm a doer, not a learner." Could he have it right? Is doctrine a drab discipline fit only for the halls of academia?

As it happens, the Bible has much to say about doctrine and only ever commends it as something that is of great importance to every Christian. In fact, we cannot rightly consider ourselves faithful followers of Jesus Christ unless we thoroughly know our doctrine, staunchly cling to it, and faithfully defend it. Though the Christian faith is far more than knowing doctrine, it is never less. And yet many who profess to be Christians have only the most rudimentary knowledge of Christian doctrine.

Many who claim to love the Bible have only the barest knowledge of the doctrines it contains. Many who have received the sacred deposit of the gospel are unequipped to guard it. And for men, who are called to lead their homes in devotion to God, the pursuit of doctrine often takes a back seat to easier, more comfortable pursuits. With the spare time before and after work, relaxing with television sounds far more appealing than laboring over the doctrine found in Scripture. But there is great cost to neglecting the study of doctrine, just as there is inestimable gain in a deep knowledge of it. To rightly pursue God for a lifetime, we must know who he is and how he calls us to live. If you are going to run to win, you must train yourself to know your doctrine.

DOCTRINE

The word *doctrine* simply refers to what the Bible teaches about a given subject. As you carefully study the Bible and recognize its themes, you come to understand what it communicates about an endless variety of subjects—the doctrine of Scripture, for example, which explains what the Bible says about itself; the doctrine of God, which describes what the Bible tells us about the nature, character, and works of God; and the doctrine of salvation, which tells us how God saves people from their sin.

The Bible divides doctrine into two broad categories:

sound and false. Sound doctrine originates in the mind of God, is consistent with the Word of God, and proves profitable to the people of God. You are responsible to know such doctrine so you can live by it and faithfully protect it. False doctrine originates outside the mind of God, is inconsistent with the Word of God, and is unprofitable to the people of God. You are responsible to reject such doctrine and to distance yourself from people who proclaim it.

While pastors are specially charged to know, promote, and defend sound doctrine, all Christians are expected to be well-versed in it. Why? Because faithfully living for God is inseparable from rightly knowing God. Those who know him best are equipped to serve him best. Those with the deepest knowledge have opportunity to express the greatest obedience.

MORE THAN FACTS

Doctrine involves facts, to be sure. But these are not cold facts accumulated in scornful minds to later be used as a kind of theological trump card. Rather, these facts are vital truths that motivate faithful lives. Married men, think of your relationship with your wife: when you were first dating her and learned about difficult events from her childhood, you gained facts that allowed you to better know and appreciate her. When you learned that your wife loves mint chocolate truffles, this is not a fact you simply filed away but one you used to express love to her. In the context of an intimate relationship, facts are not accumulated so that you can merely recite information about a person or create a page for them on Wikipedia. Facts are accumulated so that you can diligently pursue that person in love.

Similarly, when you learn facts of the Christian faith, you are gaining knowledge that allows you to better understand God so you can better pursue God. Suppose you read in Scripture of the extent of God's love for you: "In love he predestined us for adoption to himself as sons through Jesus Christ, according to the purpose of his will" (Ephesians 1:4–5). Through this verse, you come to understand that God's love for you pre-dated the creation of the world and that ultimately your salvation was the result of his determined purpose. Now you better understand the character of God (He is good! He is loving! He is powerful!), and you better understand the actions of God (He initiated! He loved! He acted!). You are growing in doctrine! Having believed these facts, you begin to live with greater confidence, knowing that your salvation is not dependent upon your will but upon God's. You begin to love God more deeply and pursue him more joyfully as a recipient of his sovereign grace. Your love for him overflows in greater patience and love for others as you long to display the same kind of love God extended to you. Those facts have now deepened your relationship and changed your life. Doctrine does not merely inform your mind but also warms your heart and reforms your behavior.

DOCTRINE AND LIFE

Few Christian men will become professional theologians and teach doctrine in classrooms and seminaries. But every

Christian man, including you, ought to aspire to be an amateur theologian, to study and to know the facts of the faith. This doctrine will equip you to live a life that is pleasing to God.

Only the husband who has deep knowledge of the ways and works of Jesus Christ is well-equipped to love his wife, "as Christ loved the church and gave himself up for her" (Ephesians 5:25). How can he love like Christ if he does not know how Christ loved? Only the father who has studied doctrine can "bring [his children] up in the discipline and instruction of the Lord" (Ephesians 6:4). How can he teach what he himself has not yet learned? Only the church member who knows his facts can serve his church as an elder, for an elder "must hold firm to the trustworthy word as taught, so that he may be able to give instruction in sound doctrine and also to rebuke those who contradict it" (Titus 1:9). Do you feel inadequate to take on leadership in your church because you don't know the doctrine necessary to lead people in the faith? Only the believer who knows the content of the faith is able to skillfully "contend for the faith that was once for all delivered to the saints" (Jude 1:3). How can you defend your faith in the workplace, how can you protect your family against Satan's attacks, how can you be a promoter of truth if you cannot distinguish sound doctrine from false?

DO IT NOW

Are you uncertain of where to begin in studying doctrine? Here are a few suggestions of basic introductions to theology:

- *Basic Christianity* by John Stott
- *Knowing God* by J.I. Packer
- *Core Christianity* by Michael Horton.

For more advanced reading, perhaps try:

- *Systematic Theology* by Wayne Grudem
- *Biblical Doctrine* by John MacArthur.

For video instruction, consider a subscription to Ligonier's Connect platform which offers a host of excellent courses on a wide variety of subjects.

RUN TO WIN!

Do you know your doctrine? Do you know at least the basic facts of the Christian faith? You have no excuse for ignorance. Of all generations, ours is most blessed in our exposure to the facts of the Christian faith. We have pastors who faithfully preach the Word and take seriously God's instruction to "be ready in season and out of season; reprove, rebuke, and exhort, with complete patience and teaching" (2 Timothy 4:2). We have countless systematic theologies written not only for theologians but for laypersons. We have a host of online courses just waiting for us. We have every opportunity and every reason to fill our minds with the knowledge of God.

To know doctrine is to know the content of the Christian faith and what is necessary to properly live it out. You cannot run well if you do not know where you are going. Your faithfulness to God depends upon your knowledge of God. Christian man, to run to win you must know your doctrine.

STRENGTH FOR THE RACE

Second Timothy 2:15 says, "Do your best to present yourself to God as one approved, a worker who has no need to be ashamed, rightly handling the word of truth." To be a good student of biblical doctrine requires some hard work—in fact, the NASB translates the beginning of that verse, "*Be diligent* to present yourself approved." Can any of us, even those who are paid to study the Bible, honestly say that we are as diligent as we could be in this pursuit? The answer is no, so we might be tempted to give up on it because we are never learning as much as we should. But Paul's command to study is bookended with words like these: "If we are faithless, he remains faithful" (v. 13) and "God's firm foundation stands, bearing this seal: the Lord knows those who are his" (v. 19). So when you feel inadequate in your knowledge of the Bible, cling to the rock of God's faithful, unfailing love for you in Christ, and let that provide the motivation you need to learn more about him from his Word.

4

PRACTICE YOUR DEVOTION

In all the books I've read, I've come to learn that the effort of reading an entire book is often rewarded with a single profound sentence. In a book made up of thousands of words, just one sentence can have the power to transform us.

I remember one such sentence in a book I read early on as a Christian on the subject of godliness. I do not remember much of its content or even its title. But I do remember one line, which was the main point of the book: *Character is who you are when no one is looking.* The author was saying that your truest self is the one that comes out when no one else is around, when you are outside the watchful eyes of your parents, your children, your wife, your friends, and your pastors. When you can do whatever you want to do, when you can say whatever you want to say, when you can look at whatever you want to look at and probably get away with it—this is who you really are. This simple sentence challenged me deeply and continues to do so today. It alone made the book worth reading.

As we strive to be men who run to win, we have to consider many contexts in which our behavior is seen and known by the public. But we also have to consider a few in which we are outside the view of anyone else. One of the things we do (or perhaps don't do) when no one is looking is private worship or personal devotions. Men, if you are going to run to win, you need to practice your devotion.

WHEN NO ONE IS LOOKING

Who are you when no one else is around? How does that compare to who you are when people are looking? Many men face the temptation to gain a reputation for their attendance and participation in public worship while remaining almost completely absent from private worship. When they attend church services they stand where they can be seen, they sing loudly, they listen attentively, they give generously. Well and good. Yet from Monday to Saturday they may rarely open their Bible and rarely close their eyes to pray. Publicly they are strong and engaged; privately they are weak and distant. Could that be true of you?

While the Bible commends public worship and demands that you prioritize attendance and participation at your local church, it also commends personal devotion. From its opening pages to its conclusion, we find God's people voluntarily relating to God as part of their private life. Adam and Eve walked and talked with God in the garden; Isaac went out into the fields to quietly meditate; David rose early to consider God's law and to pour out his praise; even Jesus was careful to carve out times of solitude in which he could commune with his Father. Who were these people when no one was looking? While only Jesus was without flaw or failing, for the most part they were, in private, the same people they were in public: worshipers. Their public reputation of godliness was rooted in a private devotion to God.

A REAL RELATIONSHIP

When you came to a saving knowledge of Jesus Christ, your sins were forgiven and you were given the sure promise of eternal life. But, amazingly, God gave you even more than that. He also gave you himself so that you entered into relationship with the living God. What is true of every relationship is true of this one—if it is to be healthy, it requires communication.

A few years ago I read a news story about a woman who decided her husband had insulted her one time too many. She decided to get revenge by giving him the ultimate silent treatment, and for several years did not utter a single word in his presence. Obviously, this was devastating to their marriage. It is impossible to sustain any relationship, especially an intimate one like that of husband and wife, without communication. It is communication that allows a relationship to begin and then thrive. A genuine, healthy relationship depends upon speaking and listening. In fact, the health of a relationship can be measured by the willingness, frequency, and depth of the speaking and listening between the two people. The healthiest relationships are those in which each speaks frequently, freely, and intimately while the other listens attentively.

On that basis, how is your relationship with God? One of the great joys of being a Christian is that you have entered into a genuine relationship with God. Our God is not merely an idea to study or a force to experience or an object to observe. God is a being to know—three persons who together are God. This God has existed eternally in that perfect relationship of Father, Son, and Holy Spirit and, through salvation, has invited you to enter in so you can know and be known by Father, Son, and Spirit. You can speak with confidence that God will hear; you can listen with confidence that God will speak. You can pour out your heart to him even as he pours out his heart to you. What a joy! What a privilege! Do you take advantage of that privilege?

God speaks today through the Bible. Its words are his words, its message his message, its power his power. Every word of the Bible is inspired and inerrant, "profitable for teaching, for reproof, for correction, and for training in righteousness, that the man of God may be complete, equipped for every good work" (2 Timothy 3:16–17). You simply cannot be a mature Christian without hearing God speak through the Bible. You cannot run well without his instruction.

We speak to God through prayer. Our words do not ascend to an empty sky but reach the ear of God, warm the heart of God, and bring about the will of God. It is God's good plan not to operate apart from prayers but through prayers since, as he promises, "the prayer of a righteous person has great power as it is working" (James 5:16). The Bible knows nothing of a Christian who does not or will not pray. You cannot run well without telling him how you are running, admitting to him when you have stumbled, and asking him for strength to run better still.

In a normal conversation, speaking and listening go together, and the same is true when conversing with God. As you read God's Word you respond in prayer—prayers of confession when he reveals sin, prayers of gratitude when you encounter his mercy, prayers of supplication when you understand how much you need his grace. And as you pray, God often brings Scripture to mind and deepens your understanding of it. Just as conversations with friends involve an organic back and forth, a mutual exchange of information and ideas, so does your communication with God. As time goes on and as you grow in your relationship, you find that God is not just your Creator and your Father, but he is also your Friend.

Men, your church, your wife, and your children need more than a man who dutifully shows up on Sunday. They need a man who knows God. They need a man who makes time to meet with God in his Word each day. And what your church, your wife, and your family need from you is exactly what God desires for you. "Thus says the Lord: 'Let not the wise man boast in his wisdom, let not the mighty man boast in his might, let not the rich man boast in his riches, but let him who boasts boast in this, that he understands and knows me'" (Jeremiah 9:23).

DO IT NOW

The time to start practicing your devotion is now. If the practice of meeting with God every day is new to you, here are a few ways to get started:

- *Resolve to make private devotion a priority in your life.* If it is a priority, you will make time for it. Resolve that the best thing—meeting with God—will come before other good things.

- *Make a plan.* Set a time when you will meet with God each day and decide where you are going to do it. In general, the things you don't plan are the things you don't do.

- *Find a Bible-reading plan.* There are dozens—perhaps hundreds—of such plans on the internet. Because you want to get a grasp of the full counsel of God, I would recommend finding a plan that goes through the whole Bible, book by book.

- *Organize your prayers.* Often the greatest difficulty to consistent, sustained prayer is simply our inability to recall what we need to pray for. I've found the Prayer-Mate app a helpful way to remember what you need to pray for each day.

- *Start small.* As you begin practicing your devotion, go for short and consistent rather than long and erratic. If you've never read the Bible daily, don't start by reading five chapters a day! If you've never prayed consistently in private, don't start by trying to pray for an hour! By

God's grace, you can work up to broader reading and more extended time in prayer. But you need to start by building the habit of devotion and then you can work your way up to strengthening the habit.

- *Persevere.* Don't be discouraged when you miss a day or even a week. Pick right back up and build the habit. Over time what seems difficult to remember and do will become as natural as breathing.

RUN TO WIN!

There are a million things competing for your time and attention, and many of these are very good things. But none are more important than your relationship with God. I trust you are involved in a local church and committed to the weekly worship services. But I hope this is not the sum of your worship, a complete accounting of your speaking to God and hearing from God. God gives you the ability to have a genuine relationship with him. He invites you to listen as he speaks and promises that as you speak he will listen to your every word. Why would you deny yourself such a privilege? If you are going to run to win, you must practice your devotion.

STRENGTH FOR THE RACE

Once Christians realize they should spend private time with the Lord on a regular basis, or "have their devotions" as it's been called, they often struggle with feelings of guilt for not doing it enough. Maybe they make a commitment to do it every day and find it difficult to follow through, and then are tempted to give up the practice entirely because they feel like they'll never measure up. The first disciples of Jesus, in the Garden of Gethsemane on the night before the Crucifixion, fell asleep twice even though the Lord himself directly commanded them to "Watch and pray that you may not enter into temptation" (Matthew 26:41). But despite this spectacular failure in their "personal devotions," at the time when Jesus needed them the most, he was understanding and tender with them when he added, "The spirit indeed is willing, but the flesh is weak." He not only freely forgave them, but he went on to use them in mighty ways in his kingdom plan, blessing them with the gift of the Holy Spirit, the call of apostleship, and the privilege of taking the gospel to the nations. He can and will bless you in your weakness as well, so don't give up!

5

PRIORITIZE YOUR CHURCH

A few years ago, Aileen and I walked into a gym for the very first time. We were unfit, we were determined to do something about it, and we had an inkling that a gym was the place to go. We spoke to the club's manager, arranged an appointment, and groaned our way through an hour-long assessment. He then assigned a trainer, who assured us he would help us melt away a few pounds and put on a bit of muscle. It actually worked! We worked with our trainer, followed his plan, and soon saw our bodies respond just the way we had hoped.

If the gym is the natural context to pursue physical fitness, the local church is the natural context to pursue spiritual fitness. The church is God's gymnasium. As a Christian man, you are running a race and, if you mean to run it well, you need training that will help you reach and maintain peak performance. It is in the local church that you encounter the trainers who instruct and guide you, that you follow the training regimen God has planned out for you. It is here that you work out alongside peers who are training for their own race so you can be inspired by their labor and so you can motivate them in return. If you are going to run to win, you need to prioritize your church.

THE PURPOSE OF THE CHURCH

The local church is central to God's plan for the world. In fact, in many ways the local church is God's plan for the world. Much of what God means to teach the world, he teaches through the local church; much of what he means to display to the world, he displays through the local church; much of what he means to accomplish in the world, he accomplishes through the local church. No ministry can outshine it, no program can replace it, no power can topple it. The local church is God's plan, and he has no backup.

God means for each Christian to be involved in a local church, and his Word knows nothing of Christians who will not be part of one. The local church welcomes into membership those who believe and puts out those who have abandoned the faith, so that each church is a community of Christians bound together by their common profession of faith.

For unbelievers, the local church serves as an outpost in enemy territory. In a world that is in outright rebellion against God, these assemblies offer the good news of reconciliation. Unbelievers are welcomed into worship services so they can experience Christian worship, hear the gospel message, profess faith in Christ, and be baptized in his name. The church exists to evangelize!

For believers, the local church serves as the spiritual health club, the place where we are trained to run our race. It is here that we learn about God so we grow in knowledge, that we worship God so we grow in love, that we are ministered to by God's people so we grow in godliness, and that we minister to others so we grow in humility. It is here that we come under the care and oversight of elders, the trainers God has specially called and equipped to model godliness and to call us to it. The church exists to edify!

While each of us competes in an individual pursuit and strives toward our prize, we do not run alone, for alongside us is a company of brothers and sisters, each laboring to win their own race. Thank God for the local church!

PRIORITIZE YOUR CHURCH

If the local church is central to God's plan for his world, it is equally central to God's plan for your life. And for that reason I must ask: What is your relationship with the local church? Are you part of a church? Are you involved in it? Are you contributing to it in meaningful ways? You cannot expect to thrive or even survive without it.

This may be hard for us to admit. We are men! We are strong and fierce and independent! But God means to teach us that we are not as strong as we might think. In fact, we are so weak that we desperately need the help of others. We need to be strengthened by the elderly, we need to be taught by the disabled, we need to be encouraged by the children, we need to be stirred by the unloved, we need to be humbled by the feeble. It is in the local church that we learn to run well.

To run well, you need the worship of the local church. It is in the weekly worship services that you sing your praise and worship to God, that you read the Bible with others, that you hear a preacher exposit a text, that you join in prayer with other Christians, and that you celebrate baptism and the Lord's Supper. These are the ordinary means of grace through which God is pleased to nourish and strengthen you, to equip you for the race.

To run well, you need the service of the local church. You need brothers and sisters who will model godliness before you, who will encourage you through times of trial, who will remind you of the gospel when you've sinned and repented, who will lovingly rebuke you when you've sinned and failed to repent. You need them to exercise their spiritual gifts for your benefit and your edification. You are weak and deeply dependent upon others.

To run well, you need to serve the local church. You may be tempted to approach church hoping that you will get a lot out of it. It is far better and far godlier to approach church asking what you will be able to give to others. Who needs you to serve them this morning? Who needs to be encouraged by your presence, by your fellowship, by your words? Instead of wondering, *How will church meet my needs?*, you ought to ask yourself, *Whose needs can I meet?* The benefit of church is not only in what you learn or what you experience, but in how you serve. Though it may seem counterintuitive, you actually run your race better when you spend time training others, when you invest in them and help them to run well.

DO IT NOW

When it comes to prioritizing church, good intentions may get you started, but it will take conviction and habit to keep you going. Let me offer a few practical tips.

- *Find a good church.* If you already attend a healthy church that proclaims the gospel, thank God for his provision. If you are attending an unhealthy church or not attending at all, helpful resources you can use to try to find one in your area include www.thegospelcoalition. org/churches, www.9marks.org/church-search, and www.tms.edu/find-a-church.

- *Go all-in.* I recently read that nearly two-thirds of all people with a gym membership no longer actually attend their gym. At one time their intentions were good, they determined they would get fit, and they signed on the dotted line. But without conviction and habit they quickly stopped. Many people are much the same with church—they have their church, but attend only occasionally and serve only sparingly. On its own, a gym membership cannot get you a fit body. You need to actually go the gym and to take advantage of its equipment and programs. Likewise, merely choosing a church will do no good for your soul. You must partici-pate in the church and take advantage of what it offers.

Find out how your church means to disciple believers, and commit to their program.

- *Structure your life around church.* Many desires, responsibilities, and hobbies that can interfere with church attendance, not the least of which is amateur sports. Make church your highest priority on a Sunday morning and, as far as possible, allow nothing to interfere. It is far better to stop chasing the dream of your child earning a football scholarship and to join him in pursuing godly character and Christian service in the local church.

- *Lead your family.* As a husband and father, you bear the ultimate responsibility to ensure your family has committed to a healthy local church and that they are actually attending. Be the one to commit to the church, be eager to attend and to serve, be the one who wakes the family on Sunday morning. Listen attentively to the sermon, worship with your whole heart, open your home to others, and expect that your family will be blessed by a father who takes the lead.

RUN TO WIN!

Human beings have developed places where we can train our bodies and train our minds. God himself has given us a place where we can train our souls, where we can learn to run the most important of all races. It is through the local church that he dispenses his most precious gifts of grace. If you are going to run to win, you must prioritize your church.

STRENGTH FOR THE RACE

A church should be "gospel-driven," meaning that an impetus for everything that happens in that church is gratitude for the grace of God in Christ, and that includes our motivation for attending and serving there. Hebrews 10:24–25 says, "Let us consider how to stir up one another to love and good works, not neglecting to meet together." That is a very clear passage about our need to be involved in a local church, but notice how the verses right before it tell us *why* we should do that:

> Since we have confidence to enter the holy places by the blood of Jesus, by the new and living way that he opened for us through the curtain, that is, through his flesh, and since we have a great priest over the house of God, let us draw near with a true heart in full assurance of faith, with our hearts sprinkled clean from an evil conscience and our bodies washed with pure water. Let us hold fast the confession of our hope without wavering, for he who promised is faithful. (Hebrews 10:19–23)

Jesus Christ lived among us and died for us even though we were not worthy or deserving of his love, so we should fellowship with and serve one another out of gratitude to him, despite the many differences between us.

6

MAINTAIN YOUR VIGILANCE

We all love to watch the occasional fail video, don't we? What started years ago on primetime television has migrated to YouTube and become one of our beloved pastimes. Some of my favorites are "finish line fails," compilations of athletes celebrating just a bit too soon.

In one of these finish line fails, an Olympic runner is nearing the end of his race, still going at a tremendous pace. He has swept around the final turn and is now just 15 or 20 meters from the finish line. Convinced that he has an insurmountable lead, he slows his pace, raises his arms in victory, and coasts toward the tape, savoring the adulation of the roaring crowd. But he has failed to keep a watchful eye on the competition, and another runner is far closer than he thinks. This second-place runner sees his opportunity. Digging deep, he summons a last reserve of energy and surges forward. Just a step from the finish line he pushes past to claim the gold, an inch ahead of the careless runner.

As a Christian man, you are running the race of life and looking forward to victory. You are running to win! But it is imperative that you do not claim victory too soon, or you will be like that embarrassed and disappointed Olympic athlete. He, too, was running to win, but he let up. He neglected to maintain his pace and neglected to watch out for the competitor who was close behind. The arms that he raised in victory soon collapsed in defeat. If you are to be victorious in your race, you must maintain your pace all the way to finish line.

So far everything we have covered in his book relates to character, to the inner man. I have encouraged you to embrace your purpose, to renew your mind, to know your doctrine, to practice your devotion, and to prioritize your church. These practices are all for growing in godliness, for exhibiting the Christ-like character God so values. In the chapters that follow this one, we will transition to the outer man, to areas related to life and relationships. But before we do that, I want to provide a sober call for watchfulness. If you are going to run to win, you need to maintain your vigilance.

MAINTAIN YOUR VIGILANCE

I've heard it said that what distinguishes a world-class athlete from the hundreds of thousands who never quite make it is situational awareness. Wayne Gretzky remains the greatest hockey player to ever lace up a pair of skates, and he often attributes his success to counsel his father gave him when he was a boy: "Skate to where the puck is going, not where it has been." This required more than sheer speed or dexterity, though

Gretzky had both in abundance. It required keen observation, constant awareness, and split-second decision-making. Gretzky had a unique sense of how players moved across the ice, how plays developed, and of where the puck would head. Most often, he would get there first, which is why he remains the all-time points leader with no close competition. It's for good reason that he's known throughout the hockey world simply as "The Great One."

If you are going to run your race successfully, you need some of that situational awareness. You need to know that you are in a grueling competition and facing constant challenges from deadly enemies. You need to know where they are most likely to attack and where you are most likely to succumb to their unrelenting temptations. You need to be vigilant, expecting waves of assault and availing yourself of the defenses available to you.

THREE DEADLY ENEMIES

There are three great enemies you can be sure you will face from now until the day you break the tape in victory: the world, the flesh, and the devil.

Maintain your vigilance against the world. We already encountered the biblical concept of "the world" when we looked at the importance of renewing your mind. The world is any system of values and way of living that opposes God and his Word and finds satisfaction in things that are temporal rather than eternal. Those who follow the patterns of the world become obsessed with "the desires of the flesh and the desires of the eyes and pride of life" (1 John 2:16). They eschew future rewards in favor of fleeting satisfaction, and prefer what they can have today to what God promises in the future. Even though you are a Christian, you remain prone to worldly desires and worldly thinking, both of which lead inevitably to worldly living. Worldliness presses in from around and surges out from within. You cannot avoid it, so you must learn to resist it. The Bible warns you not to love the world, not to befriend it, not to be conformed to it, and not to behave like it. It warns that worldliness is the very opposite of godliness.

Maintain your vigilance against the flesh. The Bible often warns against "the flesh." As a sinful human being, you are "fleshly"—you have a sinful nature that is opposed to God and craves satisfaction in that which he forbids. "Now the works of the flesh are evident," says Paul, before providing a representative list: "sexual immorality, impurity, sensuality, idolatry, sorcery, enmity, strife, jealousy, fits of anger, rivalries, dissensions, divisions, envy, drunkenness, orgies, and things like these" (Galatians 5:19–21). When you live according to the flesh, you pursue such odious things. However, when you were saved by God, you were called to live by the Spirit and to begin to display very different attributes. "But the fruit of the Spirit is love, joy, peace, patience, kindness, goodness, faithfulness, gentleness, self-control; against such things there is no law" (22–23). You have a new nature that remains locked in moral combat with the flesh so that the great battle of your life is to put the flesh to death and to come alive to the Spirit. "But I say, walk by the Spirit, and you will not gratify the desires of the flesh. For the desires of the flesh are against the Spirit, and the desires of the Spirit are against the flesh, for these are opposed to each other, to keep you from doing the things you want to do" (Galatians 5:16–17).

Maintain your vigilance against the devil. As a Christian, you are also opposed by the devil himself. "Be sober-minded; be watchful. Your adversary the devil prowls around like a roaring lion, seeking someone to devour" (1 Peter 5:8). Though the world and the flesh are powerful, they are at least inanimate. But the devil is a being who has desires and a mind and a personality. His desire is to destroy you, his mind schemes against you, and his personality is set against you. Just as he custom-crafted temptations to lead David into adultery and Peter into denial, he will custom-craft temptations suited to your weaknesses. His great desire is to promote and expose your sin, to cause you and those around you to doubt your profession of faith.

These are the deadly enemies you face every day. They are present and they are strong. Thankfully, though, God provides great defenses with which you can maintain your vigilance.

THREE GREAT DEFENSES

Maintain your vigilance through prayer. When Paul wrote about the grim reality of spiritual warfare, he instructed Christians to "put on the whole armor of God" and, after explaining the nature of this armor, concluded with a solemn charge: "[Pray] at all times in the Spirit, with all prayer and supplication. To that end, keep alert with all perseverance, making supplication for all the saints" (Ephesians 6:11, 18). Vigilance is inseparable from prayer, which is why in another place he says, "Continue steadfastly in prayer, being watchful in it with thanksgiving" (Colossians 4:2). Jesus himself told us to pray, "Lead us not into temptation, but deliver us from evil" (Matthew 6:13). Prayer is our first great defense against the world, the flesh, and the devil. Pray that God would protect you from their encroachment, and pray equally that he would expose and correct any of your particular temptations to sin.

Maintain your vigilance through self-examination. A second defense against your enemies is self-examination. This is using God's Word to realistically assess your desires, your temptations, your habits, and your sanctification. You must do this in the light of Scripture, for only it "is living and active, sharper than any two-edged sword, piercing to the division of soul and of spirit, of joints and of marrow, and discerning the thoughts and intentions of the heart" (Hebrews 4:12). God's Word tells you what is true about yourself, and you are responsible to heed its warnings.

Maintain your vigilance through the means of grace. God extends his grace to his people through very ordinary means. It is his good will to conform you to his image and maintain you in that image through Word, prayer, and fellowship. You must read the Word and pray in your home and in your church, in the quietness of your devotions and the chaos of your family, until you can truly say you are "constant in prayer" (Romans

12:12). You must enjoy Christian fellowship, primarily in the local church, gathering together to worship, to serve, to hear the Word preached, and to participate in baptism and the Lord's Supper. You can trust that it is God's good pleasure to work through ordinary means to bring about extraordinary holiness. You cannot expect to thrive in the Christian life or to survive the onslaughts of your enemies if you neglect these most important means.

DO IT NOW

It is a negligent soldier who neglects his duty to watch when he knows the enemy is nearby. Your enemy is approaching right now, so here are a few ways to get started and then to persevere in vigilance.

- *Pray.* Pray and pray and pray.
- *Know your areas of temptation.* Where you have experienced and succumbed to temptation before, you are likely to experience it again. You will probably succumb to it again if you have not addressed that weakness of character.
- *Enlist an ally.* Tell your spouse or a friend where you battle temptation and enlist them to pray for you and to ask you probing questions. Commit to always answer those questions honestly. In the area of sexual sin and temptation, you will probably benefit from regularly confiding in a brother and allowing him to speak truth into your life.

- ***Trust the means of grace.*** Trust that God has appointed these means rather than others to promote zeal for godliness, to foster godliness, and to preserve godliness to the end. Trust them and take full advantage of them.
- ***Prioritize the Lord's Supper.*** Make the celebration of the Lord's Supper a special time of self-examination. When you know it is approaching, take the time to carefully examine yourself according to the Bible's instruction: "Let a person examine himself, then, and so eat of the bread and drink of the cup" (1 Corinthians 11:28).

RUN TO WIN!

It is both foolish and perilous to celebrate too early. The world, the flesh, and the devil thrive where there is apathy or pride, where you do not care to maintain watchfulness or where you do not consider it necessary. Conversely, these enemies wither before prayer, self-examination, and the ordinary means of grace. Until the day you are in the presence of the Lord, you must keep up your pace and keep a close eye on your enemies. If you are going to run to win, you must maintain your vigilance.

STRENGTH FOR THE RACE

Perseverance in the faith requires divine grace as much or more than any other endeavor, because anyone can start well and run fast for a while, but to finish the race requires an extra measure of spiritual energy. That power to persevere comes from the grace of God working through the gospel truths of his love for us. Hebrews 10:23 says, "Let us hold fast the confession of our hope without wavering, *for he who promised is faithful*." And 1 John 2:24–25 says, "Let what you heard from the beginning abide in you. If what you heard from the beginning abides in you, then you too will abide in the Son and in the Father. And *this is the promise that he made to us*—eternal life." The faithful promises of God, especially those related to the new life we have in Christ and the next life we'll enjoy with him in heaven, provide the strength we need to maintain spiritual vigilance to the end of our time on earth.

PART 2

DISCIPLINES OF LIFE

7

REDEEM YOUR TIME

Is there anything more tragic than the passage of time? Is there anything that brings about deeper grief than seeing time pass us by, than acknowledging how much has already elapsed and how little remains? We who were made to live *forever* are now given mere decades. "If a person lives many years, let him rejoice in them all," says wise old Solomon, "but let him remember that the days of darkness will be many. All that comes is vanity" (Ecclesiastes 11:8).

Christian men, you have been given a race to run, and you have been called to run to win. At times this race will seem like a marathon and at times a sprint. During times of sorrow or adversity, the days may seem to drag, each one bearing the weight of a lifetime, grueling days giving way to long, sleepless nights. But during times of joy the days will fly by, and you will marvel at how quickly time has passed. An Olympic sprinter spends years in training to prepare for an event that is over in ten seconds. At times it will seem like your life has gone by just as quickly, that the child you were only just cradling in your arms is now holding your arm as you escort her down the aisle. Whether life plods by or speeds by, you are responsible for each moment. If you are going to run to win, you must redeem your time.

REDEEM THE TIME

There is nothing you have that has not been given to you, no good thing you possess that is not a gift of God's grace. You who deserve only wrath and condemnation have been given innumerable blessings. You are responsible before God to faithfully steward each one of them. If God has given you the blessing of marriage, you must always keep in mind that your wife is first God's daughter, his creation. Your foremost responsibility is to care for her in a way that honors and pleases the Father. If God has given you children, they are first his children, created in his image and for his glory. The call of a father is to discipline and instruct his children on behalf of God. If God has given you money, it is his money, and you are meant to use it as if God is going to require an accounting for every penny. What is true of a wife and children and money is true of time. Yet, as Donald Whitney says, "If people threw away their money as thoughtlessly as they throw away their time, we would think them insane." [1]

God has given you the gift of time, and he has given it to you in trust with the expectation that you will use it wisely and that you will diligently commit it to the highest of purposes. When Paul writes to the church in Ephesus, he calls them to live lives of extraordinary holiness, then says, "Look carefully then how you walk, not as unwise but as wise, making the best use of the time, because the days are evil" (Ephesians 5:15–16). "Making the best use of time" is, more literally, "redeeming the time" (KJV). Time must be redeemed by liberating it from useless pursuits and dedicating it to the highest purposes. Time is laid out before you, and it must be grasped, it must be seized from all the ignoble purposes that could otherwise steal and waste it. You relate to time well when you understand it as a precious gift to be used, not a valueless possession to be squandered.

God knows the number of years, months, and days he has allocated to you. You cannot add to or take away from them. But what you can do in greater or lesser measure is put that time to use. While still a young man, Jonathan Edwards resolved "never to lose one moment of time; but improve it the most profitable way I possibly can." He understood that time had been given to him in trust, and he meant to use it well. He, like the wise and loyal servant in Jesus' parable of the talents, longed to hear, "Well done, good and faithful servant. You have been faithful over a little; I will set you over much. Enter into the joy of your master" (Matthew 25:21).

TIME WASTED, TIME REDEEMED

Time is a gift you are meant to accept and treasure. Yet there are many things competing for your time, many temptations to misuse it. Let's consider a few common ways time can be wasted.

You waste time in laziness. If Solomon so regularly warned of laziness in his day, how much more do we need to guard against it in a world of endless entertainment and ubiquitous social media? The lazy man is the one who makes any excuse not to work, the one who irresponsibly lies in bed or on the sofa when there is work that needs to be done, the one who begins projects but never brings them to completion, the one who cannot learn because he considers himself surpassingly wise (Proverbs 26:13–16). Your mother may have warned you that "idle hands are the devil's workshop." Behind the cliché is a sober warning, for those who pass their days in idleness are those who practically beg Satan to tempt them to sin.

You waste time in busyness. Busyness is a cousin to laziness and no more noble than its relative. It is a modern-day plague. Even if you reject laziness, you may swing to the opposite pole of busyness, filling your every moment with activity and judging yourself by the number of tasks completed. Today you practically expect that when you ask a friend how he is doing he will reply, "Busy! So busy!" Yet busyness must not be confused with diligence, the number of activities with meaningful accomplishments. God has given you a short little life and expects that, of all the great things you could do, you will identify and pursue the few that matter most. Because there is only so much you can do, diligence and redeeming the time involves saying "no" to a million good opportunities to focus fully on a few excellent ones.

You waste time in spiritual carelessness. It was Martin Luther who famously said his busiest times also needed to be his most prayerful. When responsibilities threatened to overwhelm him, he knew that he was too busy not to pray. You fail to redeem your time when you fail to prioritize your spiritual growth and health. If life is too busy for you to read God's Word, to spend time in prayer, and to attend the local church, it is far too busy. If you are too unmotivated to commit to such basic disciplines, you are in spiritual peril. Before you do anything else, take a step out from the whirlwind of busyness and reassess your priorities in light of eternity.

You waste time when you do not rest. God himself chose to work for six days, then to rest for one. He did this not because he was worn out, but to set a pattern that we would follow. We are weak and limited creatures who need to rest. Our need for rest requires that we commit enough of our time to sleep and to activities that will refresh our minds and spirits. Rest and recreation are necessary to renew us and to prepare us to diligently carry out the tasks God has assigned to us.

DO IT NOW

Right now is the time to redeem your time! Consider how you can commit to diligently steward your moments and your days.

- *Pursue and grasp a biblical understanding of productivity.* Properly understood, productivity is not "getting lots done" or "getting more done than the other guy." Productivity is using your gifts, talents, time, energy, and enthusiasm for the good of others and the glory of God.

A biblical understanding of productivity will free you from lesser pursuits and help you focus on the ones that matter most.

- *Plan to be disciplined.* It is very telling that when we are busy or lazy, the spiritual disciplines tend to be among the first things we neglect. Be sure you plan the time, place, and context in which you will read God's Word and pray every day. Be sure you prioritize worshiping with the local church and never allow anything to supplant it. And then, once you have put first things first, plan how and when you will do your most meaningful work throughout the week.

- *Resolve to constrain or cut out enemies of your diligence.* In our day, there is no shortage of distractions eager to bring you from meaningful labor into meaningless sloth. What needs to be cut out or significantly restricted from your life in order for you to redeem the time? Do you need to limit Netflix or other viewing time so that you can spend more time connecting with your wife and children? Do you need to delete social media apps that lure you away from diligence throughout the day? If you are going to run to win, you need to remove whatever is slowing you down.

- *Speak to someone who does it well.* We have all encountered people who model the faithful use of time. Find one of these people and ask him how and why he does it. Ask for practical pointers on using time diligently.

RUN TO WIN!

You came into this world with nothing and will leave this world with nothing. All that you have between the beginning and the end is a gift of God's grace, and that includes the little dash on your tombstone. That simple line will represent the time given to you. It was given in trust with the expectation that you would take hold of it and put it to the best and highest use. If you are going to run to win, you must redeem your time.

STRENGTH FOR THE RACE

Like the book of Romans, Ephesians starts with extensive discussions of what God has done for us—those gospel promises that we call "the doctrines of grace"—before it ever gets to what we should do for God. So you can't "redeem the time" as it says in Ephesians 5:16 (KJV) without understanding and remembering these great truths from chapters 1 through 3.

- *He predestined* us before the foundation of the world, a choice which was based solely on his sovereign love and not on any worthiness on our part (Ephesians 1:3–11).

- *He gave us new life* when we were spiritually dead and incapable of saving ourselves (Ephesians 2:1–10).

- *He made peace* through the cross so that there will never be any more hostility between him and us (Ephesians 2:11–22).

- And *he gave us an eternal inheritance*, making us beneficiaries and "partakers of the promise in Christ Jesus through the gospel" (Ephesians 3:1–13).

Making the best use of our time might be one of the hardest things we are called to do in the Christian life, but in his prayer at the end of the doctrinal section in Ephesians, Paul tells us about the sources of our strength:

> For this reason I bow my knees before the Father, from whom every family in heaven and on earth is named, that according to the riches of his glory he may grant you to be *strengthened with power* through his Spirit in your inner being, so that Christ may dwell in your hearts through faith—that you, being rooted and grounded in love, may have *strength to comprehend* with all the saints what is the breadth and length and height and depth, and to know the love of Christ that surpasses knowledge, that you may be filled with all the fullness of God. Now to him who is able to do far more abundantly than all that we ask or think, according to the *power at work within us*, to him be glory in the church and in Christ Jesus throughout all generations, forever and ever. Amen. (Ephesians 3:14–21)

8

ACT YOUR AGE!

"I just don't know if I'm ready to settle down yet." He had recently celebrated his 30th birthday but was still content to live in his parents' home, to eat their food, to enjoy their rent-free accommodations. He told me how he enjoyed his girlfriend and sometimes joined her in her parents' home for weeks or even months at a time, but he still wasn't quite ready to go to the next level by purchasing that engagement ring. Kids were in the future, too, but only off in the hazy distance. In the meantime, he was working his way up from part-time to full-time work, but thinking of going back to school to pursue a different career. That would be tough, though, because he had a passion for video games and wouldn't want to get so busy that he couldn't give them time.

It all sounds so cliché, so Millennial, but this was a real conversation with a real 30-year-old man; I haven't exaggerated a word. He was growing older, but not growing up; progressing in years, but years behind in maturity. In an age of immaturity, it's imperative that every Christian man grow up. My friend, if you are going to run to win, you need to act your age.

MILK TO MEAT

The Bible has a lot to say about maturity. While much of its instruction is in the context of spiritual maturity, there is a close correlation between maturity of faith and maturity of life. The man who lives a childish life is unlikely to possess spiritual maturity or display mature character.

In Paul's first letter to Timothy, he exhorts him in this way: "Let no one despise you for your youth, but set the believers an example in speech, in conduct, in love, in faith, in purity" (1 Timothy 4:12). The old mentor wrote to his young protégé to encourage him to display a maturity beyond his years. While church and society may have had low expectations of young men, Paul's were very high. In fact, Timothy was to be exemplary in his maturity, to behave in such a mature way that he would set an example even to those much older than himself. The young are to chart the way for the old.

When the author of Hebrews wrote to his congregation, he expressed concern for their lack of spiritual maturity. These people had once been making good progress and growing steadily, but something had gone wrong. Their maturity first plateaued and then went into decline, so he could rightly say, "For though by this time you ought to be teachers, you need someone to teach you again the basic principles of the oracles of God" (5:12a). His appropriate and realistic expectation was steady, lifelong progress, but their maturity had slowed, halted, and declined. "You need milk, not solid food," he said, "for everyone who lives on milk is unskilled in the word of righteousness, since he is a child. But solid food is for the mature, for those who have their powers of discernment trained by constant practice to distinguish good from evil. Therefore let us leave the elementary doctrine of Christ and go on to maturity." (5:12b—6:1). Their immature doctrine was leading to immature living, and this was a source of deep grief to their pastor and their God.

This theme of maturity shows up elsewhere in Paul's letters and also in Peter's. It becomes clear that progressing from infancy to adulthood, from childishness to maturity, is a prominent theme in the Bible. God has created us in such a way that as we progress in years, we are to progress in maturity. Our challenge is to accept and pursue the responsibilities that come with each stage of life. No matter your age, you need to act your age.

NO ROOM FOR IMMATURITY

Some of what it means to be mature is conditioned by culture. In pre-industrial, agrarian societies, children needed to grow up quickly so they could get to work and provide for their family. They were considered adults early because at a young age they took their place doing adult activities. As society developed and wealth grew, children had the privilege of extending childhood while they attended school, then college. In an extravagant and pampered society like our own, adults can remain children almost indefinitely, which is why some studies now suggest that adolescence begins at 12 and stretches to 32.

In the face of this cultural embrace of immaturity, Christians bear the responsibility of growing up. No matter your age, you are responsible before God to act your age and to prepare yourself to act the next age. The Bible allows no room for complacency, no room for immaturity.

In Paul's letter to Titus, he gives age- and gender-specific instructions to four groups of people: young women, older women, young men, and older men. It is noteworthy that while he provides a whole list of instructions to the other three groups, he has just one instruction for young men: "Urge the younger men to be self-controlled" (Titus 2:6). Self-control perfectly addresses immaturity. It is immaturity that keeps men endlessly glued to video games instead of enjoying them in moderation. It is immaturity that keeps young men obsessed with pornography instead of living in purity, pursuing a bride, and finding delight in her body (Proverbs 5:18–19). It is immaturity that traps men in fear and apathy and keeps them from making bold decisions and taking big steps. Immaturity is a modern-day plague. For younger men, the path out of immaturity is the path of self-control.

For older men, there is a little bit more to maturity: "Older men are to be sober-minded, dignified, self-controlled, sound in faith, in love, and in steadfastness" (Titus 2:2). Having progressed in years, ability, character, and godliness, older men are to cast aside all that hinders their growth and press on until the very end. Greater age actually brings greater responsibility, for they are now responsible not only for their own development, but for the development of younger men. Just as a great runner holds back a burst of speed for the last few feet of his race, a godly man makes his final years the ones in which he displays a final burst of maturity.

DO IT NOW

Here are some tips on getting started.

- *Consider your age.* What responsibilities come with your age? What responsibilities ought to come with your age? Honestly assess whether you are displaying maturity in your actions and your character. Honestly assess if you are mature in what you are doing and how you are living.

- *Consider your passions.* Few pursuits and activities are immature in and of themselves. "For everything created by God is good, and nothing is to be rejected if it is received with thanksgiving" (1 Timothy 4:4). Rather, immaturity expresses itself in putting undue time, attention, or money into lesser things. It is good to have a hobby, but a hobby should never compete with more important responsibilities like family, church, and vocation. Consider what you are passionate about and whether you are allowing lesser things to have undue prominence.

- *Commit to lifelong growth.* A runner can't stop competing until he has crossed the finish line, and a Christian can't stop maturing until he has crossed into heaven. You need to make a lifelong commitment to increasing maturity. Commit today that you will embrace your current stage in life and every responsibility that comes with it.

- *Mature in every way.* One aspect of maturity cannot easily be isolated from others. You cannot expect to grow in your faith or character while you content yourself to remain immature in your time and activities. Ensure that you are pursuing and achieving greater measures of maturity in all areas of life, not just one or two.

RUN TO WIN!

God expects that you will make growth in maturity a priority at every age and at every stage of life. While immaturity may offer the illusion of ease and comfort, it over-promises and under-delivers. It actually keeps you from doing what God means for you to do and being who God means for you to be. If you are going to run to win, you are going to need to act your age.

STRENGTH FOR THE RACE

What is the key to Christian maturity? Or I should say, *Who* is the key? The answer is "Christ in you, the hope of glory," as Paul writes in Colossians 1:28: "Him we proclaim, warning everyone and teaching everyone with all wisdom, that we may present everyone mature in Christ. For this I toil, struggling with all his energy that he powerfully works within me." Whatever stage of life you are in, knowing Christ and being empowered by his Spirit is the only way to become a mature man, and it is the only effective incentive for maturing in him. We "grow in the grace and knowledge of our Lord and Savior Jesus Christ," according to Paul's fellow apostle Peter (2 Peter 3:18).

Also, as a friend of mine often says, "The greatest test of maturity is how we respond to criticism." Anyone can talk a good talk and even, to a degree, walk a good walk (when it comes to outward actions). Anyone can pray and worship with passion and apparent sincerity. But only the mature are able to respond to criticism with appreciation, self-evaluation, and humble improvement. That is because they know who they are in Christ—undeserving sinners saved by grace. They are not surprised or devastated when their sins are pointed out, nor do they find it necessary to become defensive or insult those who criticize them. If you "grow in the grace and knowledge of our Lord and Savior Jesus Christ" consistently over time, you will possess true humility and display the maturity suited to a man your age.

9

PURSUE YOUR VOCATION

Why do we work? For five or six days of every week, most of us spend at least half of our waking hours doing a job. We take time away from our families and away from worldly pleasures to pursue an occupation. It's simply what humans do. But why?

Some say we work so that we don't have to work. Best-selling books teach us how to "escape the 9-to-5," to get rich fast and set ourselves up for decades of work-free vacation at the end of our lives. We work as much as possible now so that we can work as little as possible in retirement. Others say that work is merely for provision. Work simply pays the bills and puts food on the table. In this view, work has little value apart from its material rewards.

These reasons for work aren't entirely wrong. It is wise to work now to prepare for years ahead when we will not be able to work. It is good, as we will see, to work hard to provide for our families and others in our community. But these reasons alone are insufficient. When we look at God's design for us and our work, we see that we work because we were made to work.

Here in part two of this book, we are exploring godly disciplines for Christian men. And my friend, if you are going to run to win, you must discipline yourself to pursue your vocation.

FALLEN WORK

God made you to work. Your creation and function are inextricably linked. At the very moment God announced his intention to create humanity, he described the function we would carry out in his world: "Then God said, 'Let us make man in our image, after our likeness. And let them have dominion over the fish of the sea and over the birds of the heavens and over the livestock and over all the earth and over every creeping thing that creeps on the earth'" (Genesis 1:26). You were created to carry out the important task of working in God's world as God's representative.

The work God gave to humanity was good and dignified. He gave the tasks of exploring his creation, of discovering and exploiting its resources, and of spreading across it. Humans were to form families and plant churches and found cities and build civilizations. They were to establish universities and begin businesses and invent technologies. They were to use their God-given creativity and ingenuity to exercise dominion. What had been created in an incomplete or unfinished state was to be brought to completion by mankind. Man was to bring order to chaos, to begin in that small garden and to widen its borders until the whole world was under dominion.

In a perfect world, work was easy and fulfilling. But the world would not remain perfect for long. Sin soon interfered, and now the work God had assigned in a sinless world would be carried out in one transformed by depravity. Because of sin, work became grueling instead of fulfilling.

> Because you have listened to the voice of your wife and have eaten of the tree of which I commanded you, "You shall not eat of it," cursed is the ground because of you; in pain you shall eat of it all the days of your life; thorns and thistles it shall bring forth for you; and you shall eat the plants of the field. By the sweat of your face you shall eat bread, till you return to the ground, for out of it you were taken; for you are dust, and to dust you shall return. (Genesis 3:17–19)

Work that had once been easy would now be difficult. Thorns and thistles would compete with the farmer's crops, tired eyes and disobedient minds would compete with the teacher's lessons, interruptions and fatigue would compete with the writer's words. Work was still necessary and labor still dignified, but it would be backbreaking and exasperating.

In a perfect world, work would represent and glorify God. But soon after sin entered the world, work became a source of pride, envy, and hatred (Genesis 4:3–7). Instead of using work to serve others, humans began crushing others with work (Exodus 1:11). They idolized work, living in bondage to its reward (Matthew 6:24). Or they avoided work, choosing the comforts of idleness over thorns and thistles (2 Thessalonians 3:6).

WORK REDEEMED

Yet the world's sin did not nullify God's design. Even in this sinful world, the dignity and necessity of labor remain. Even in this sinful world, work has three great and important purposes: obedience, provision, and service.

You obey through your work. The mandate God assigned humanity at creation remains in effect. You are still to exercise dominion over this earth, finding appropriate balance between exploiting its riches and caring for its beauties. Through every legitimate occupation, you obey God and carry out his mandate. As you faithfully pursue your vocation, you are acting as God's representative throughout the earth, displaying his creative power and authority.

You provide through your work. Through work, you provide for your own needs and the needs of others. As a man, you are expected to care for yourself, your family, and your church. God calls you to provide by working hard and avoiding idleness. In Paul's day, the congregation in Thessalonica was known for having a problem with people who were content to be idle. So Paul wrote to them: "Aspire to live quietly, and to mind your own affairs, and to work with your hands, as we instructed you" (1 Thessalonians 4:11). The matter of provision is a very serious one. In his second letter to the Thessalonians, Paul ramped up his rhetoric: "If anyone is not willing to work, let him not eat" (2 Thessalonians 3:10). When he wrote to Timothy, he said, "if anyone does not provide for his relatives, and especially for members of his household, he has denied the faith and is worse than an unbeliever" (1 Timothy 5:8). As a Christian man, you bear the weighty responsibility of hard work. You are to make every effort to earn enough to provide for your own needs, for the needs of those who are dependent upon you, and even enough to share with those in need. This is a sacred calling from God himself.

You serve through your work. It is through vocation that God dispenses his gifts to the world. Through the farmer he provides food, through the doctor he provides medical care, through the teacher he provides knowledge. The word *vocation* signifies that God calls each of us to different work and that all work is equally dignified if it is done to his glory. God has not only given you skills so that you can provide for your family and the church. He has also given you skills so that you can bless others who need your service. This means that if you are in a job that provides some kind of service or good to others, you don't have to leave your work in order to serve God. Run to win, and use every hour of your workweek to glorify God.

DO IT NOW

Here are a few tips on getting started in this.

- *Get to work!* You were made to work. You were made to represent God on earth, to provide for your family, and to serve others. The first step to pursuing your vocation is ensuring that you are avoiding idleness and obeying God through hard work. Of course, many men go through seasons of unemployment, sickness, or schooling that will prevent them from employment. But the biblical standard held before you is that you give yourself to hard work.

- *Serve others in your work.* Tim Keller gives helpful questions for discerning how to serve others in your work: "What opportunities are there in my profession for serving individual people, for serving society at large, for serving my field of work, for modeling competence and excellence, and for witnessing to Christ?"[2] Jot down answers to these questions and resolve to approach work with a heart of service. If you are in a job that harms people rather than helps them, or a job that offers no good or service to people, you may want to reconsider your vocation.

- *Avoid idleness.* As we saw in the chapter "Redeem Your Time," idleness is a plague today and a means through which Satan tempts you to sin. Learn the value of labor, learn to enjoy labor, and cut out any distractions that pull you into idleness. When we spend our working hours scrolling through social media instead of serving others, we are disobeying the mandate God has given us.

- *Begin to plan life after your career.* Many people work hard for the 40 or 50 years of their career but put little thought into what they will do when that work is done. Because God's design for work is more than provision, your call to work remains even if all your financial needs are met in retirement. In fact, in retirement you will likely have more time than ever to serve others and advance God's kingdom. Begin to plan now how you will adapt your vocation and avoid idleness in the years following retirement.

RUN TO WIN!

When we consider vocation and hard work, we cannot neglect to consider Jesus. When we think of him, we rightly consider the few years of his public ministry. But we should not forget that while he spent three years in the public eye, he spent 30 working in the family business. Before he was a preacher and teacher, he was a carpenter. When he finally emerged and began to teach, his perplexed neighbors asked, "Is not this the carpenter, the son of Mary and brother of James and Joses and Judas and Simon?" (Mark 6:3). And when he began his public ministry, he carried it out perfectly despite agonizing hardships. He continued to labor until his Father was satisfied and his work was complete. He is our great example. If you are going to run to win, you, like Jesus, must pursue your vocation.

STRENGTH FOR THE RACE

Notice the kinds of incentives mentioned in the two most direct New Testament passages about work. In Ephesians 6:5–8 Paul says,

> Obey your earthly masters with fear and trembling, with a sincere heart, *as you would Christ*, not by the way of eye-service, as people-pleasers, but *as bond-servants of Christ, doing the will of God* from the heart, rendering service with a good will *as to the Lord* and not to man, knowing that whatever good anyone does, this *he will receive back from the Lord*.

And in Colossians 3:23–24 he adds, "Whatever you do, work heartily, *as for the Lord* and not for men, knowing that *from the Lord* you will receive the inheritance as your reward. *You are serving the Lord Christ*." The idea of serving Christ reminds us of his words in Matthew 20:28: "The Son of Man came not to be served but to serve, and to give his life as a ransom for many." That saying contains two wonderful truths that apply to our work: we can be forgiven no matter how many times we've fallen short, because Jesus paid the price for all our sins; and we should be motivated to work harder for the one who gave his life for us!

10

MASTER YOUR FINANCES

I have a love-hate relationship with money. I love the good things money can accomplish. I love how it can be used to provide for my needs and the needs of my wife and children. I love how it can be used to support God's work in the world. I love being the contributor and the recipient of financial generosity—there is much joy in cheerful giving and grateful receiving. Yet I hate the way money can hold me captive, the way it subtly promises what only God can deliver. I hate how quickly it leaves my hands in an endless torrent of bills, payments, and expenses. Money is a joy and money is a burden.

We have been learning that victoriously running the race of life involves a wide array of skills and character traits. To our growing list we now add this: If you are going to run to win, you need to master your finances.

WHAT YOU OWN

The bank account may be in your name, but it's not actually your money. The deed to your home may have your first and last name printed at the top, but your house doesn't truly belong to you (or even to the bank). You came into this world naked and empty-handed, and you'll leave this world naked and empty-handed. All that you enjoy between birth and death is a gift. It belongs to God but is assigned to your care.

This is known as stewardship. God is the creator of all that is and, therefore, God is the owner of all that is. "The earth is the Lord's and the fullness thereof, the world and those who dwell therein" (Psalm 24:1). He owns your home, your car, your money, and everything else. You relate to these things as a steward, as one who has been given the responsibility to use them on behalf of the owner. A steward is a manager, a person responsible for the wise and skillful management of resources.

Jesus illustrated the stewardship principle in one of his best-known parables, the one we know today as the "Parable of the Talents." He tells the story of a master who is going on a journey, and before he departs, he distributes his wealth to his servants for safekeeping. To one he gives five talents, to another two, and to another one. Then he goes away, and the servants set to work. Two of the servants use the money wisely and double it; one of them buries it in the ground. When the master returns he demands an accounting. The two who have shown wisdom are rewarded, while the one who had been frugal yet unwise is rebuked. Jesus provides this application: "For to everyone who has will more be given, and he will have an abundance. But from the one who has not, even what he has will be taken away" (Matthew 25:29).

RIGHTS AND RESPONSIBILITIES

God owns all things and distributes things to you so you can use them well and wisely. All money is God's money, and while he has rights over it, you have responsibilities. He answers to no one, but you answer to him. You bear the responsibility not to squander your money, not to use it in ways that fail to carry out his purposes or even contradict his purposes. Conversely, you are responsible before God to use your money in ways that are pleasing to him, in ways that carry out his will on earth. God gives every dollar in trust and has the right to demand an accounting for it.

This is a weighty and sacred responsibility. You might think, then, that the only noble purposes for money are giving it to churches and charities and Christian ministries. But it is not so simple. God is a loving Father who "richly provides us with everything to enjoy" (1 Timothy 6:17). He does not equate stewardship with austerity. Rather, he instructs you to find an appropriate balance between what you keep and what you give, between what you use for purposes of comfort and what you use for purposes of kingdom advancement.

God addresses your heart's relationship with money both negatively and positively. Negatively, he warns you that "the love of money is a root of all kinds of evils" (1 Timothy 6:10) and insists that money offers more than it can deliver: "He

91

who loves money will not be satisfied with money, nor he who loves wealth with his income; this also is vanity" (Ecclesiastes 5:10). You must be very careful with money, knowing that it has the power to hold you captive.

Positively, God promises joy to those who hold their money loosely and give with generosity. Solomon observes, "One gives freely, yet grows all the richer; another withholds what he should give, and only suffers want. Whoever brings blessing will be enriched, and one who waters will himself be watered" (Proverbs 11:24–25). There is also joy to be had beyond this life, for even though you cannot take your wealth with you, you can, in a sense, send it on ahead (as Randy Alcorn is so fond of saying). "Sell your possessions, and give to the needy. Provide yourselves with moneybags that do not grow old, with a treasure in the heavens that does not fail, where no thief approaches and no moth destroys" (Luke 12:33). Those with wealth are "to do good, to be rich in good works, to be generous and ready to share, thus storing up treasure for themselves as a good foundation for the future, so that they may take hold of that which is truly life" (1 Timothy 6:18–19).

God has given you money so you can put it to work in his world and for his purposes. This will involve the day-to-day financial management of paying bills, buying groceries, and making payments into a retirement account. It will also involve giving generously to the church and to believers who have needs. It will involve a constant awareness that money is a wonderful servant but a terrible master, that it all belongs to God, and that it is to be used to bring glory to him.

DO IT NOW

If you are going to master your finances, you need to take action. Here are some places to begin.

- *Read a good book on money.* Few of us are taught financial management in school, in church, or in our homes. Thankfully, we are well-served with excellent books that explain God's view on money. Perhaps begin with *Managing God's Money* by Randy Alcorn, a personal favorite and an excellent primer on the subject.

- *Budget your money.* Few things make a bigger difference to your diligent stewardship of money than maintaining a budget. There are hundreds of different ways to maintain a budget, but the important principle is this: account for every penny. A good budget will force you to understand how you spend your money and call you to account for where you are spending poorly. When it comes to budgeting, that you do it is far more important than how you do it.

- *Enjoy your money.* God calls you to be a faithful steward of your money, and he is pleased when you enjoy it. As Solomon says, "Everyone also to whom God has given wealth and possessions and power to enjoy them, and to accept his lot and rejoice in his toil—this is the gift of God" (Ecclesiastes 5:19). You can buy items that make you comfortable and travel to places that are restful. Sometimes the wisest way to spend money is to spend it on something that brings you joy and blessing.

- *Ask questions.* Consider the four questions John Wesley asked of any expenditure: In spending this money, am I acting as if I own it, or am I acting as the Lord's trustee? What Scripture passage requires me to spend this money in this way? Can I offer up this purchase as a sacrifice to the Lord? Will God reward me for this expenditure at the resurrection of the just?

- *Plan your giving.* Many people form a plan to increase their retirement savings or to increase the amount they are saving for a new car. Few people plan to increase their giving to God's work. Consider how you will give more next year than you did this year. Why not plan to add a small percentage each year? If you give $200 a month this year, plan how you can make it $220 a month next year. If you give $1500 a month this year, make every effort to up it to $1600 next year. Don't allow your income and expenses to grow without also growing your giving.

RUN TO WIN!

You, like me, may have a love-hate relationship with money. You may love all the good it does and dread all the evil it causes. It helps to know that the hand of God is behind our money: "Beware lest you say in your heart, 'My power and the might of my hand have gotten me this wealth.' You shall remember the LORD your God, for it is he who gives you power to get wealth" (Deuteronomy 8:17–18). Your money is actually God's money, and through the Holy Spirit he equips you to use it well, to steward it faithfully, to someday hear the words of the grateful master: "Well done, good and faithful servant. You have been faithful over a little; I will set you over much. Enter into the joy of your master" (Matthew 25:23). In the meantime, if you are going to run to win, you must master your finances.

STRENGTH FOR THE RACE

"For you know the grace of our Lord Jesus Christ, that though he was rich, yet for your sake he became poor, so that you by his poverty might become rich" (2 Corinthians 8:9). That is a promise of spiritual riches, of course, but it is given to provide motivation for us to manage our money well and give generously to the Lord (the context is an offering for the poor that Paul was collecting from the churches). Christ's sacrifice for us not only gives us a reason to save and give our money, but it also provides hope for when we are in financial trouble, even if our own bad choices are a part of the cause. He died for all our sins, including our bad stewardship, and this other wonderful promise of his applies to all who believe:

> Do not be anxious about your life, what you will eat, nor about your body, what you will put on. For life is more than food, and the body more than clothing. Consider the ravens: they neither sow nor reap, they have neither storehouse nor barn, and yet God feeds them. Of how much more value are you than the birds! And which of you by being anxious can add a single hour to his span of life? If then you are not able to do as small a thing as that, why are you anxious about the rest? Consider the lilies, how they

grow: they neither toil nor spin, yet I tell you, even Solomon in all his glory was not arrayed like one of these. But if God so clothes the grass, which is alive in the field today, and tomorrow is thrown into the oven, how much more will he clothe you, O you of little faith! And do not seek what you are to eat and what you are to drink, nor be worried. For all the nations of the world seek after these things, and your Father knows that you need them. Instead, seek his kingdom, and these things will be added to you. (Luke 12:22–31)

11

GUARD YOUR HEALTH

As a young man, I often heard older people talking about their declining bodies and failing health. I grew weary of hearing them tell how their strength had diminished and how their aches and pains had increased. They insisted that they used to be able to eat anything they wanted without ill effect, but now practically every food gave them indigestion. Whereas they once had the ability to sleep soundly under any conditions, now any unusual circumstance would keep them lying awake long into the night.

I was convinced all of this was just idle grumbling. But then I hit my mid-30s and began to notice I wasn't recovering from activity as quickly as I did before, that I was spending more and more nights staring at the ceiling wishing I was fast asleep. I hit 40 and found that some of my favorite foods didn't sit well anymore. It was then that I realized I was not going to be the exception. I, too, was going to experience a long decline in my health and a long diminishment in my abilities. I, too, was going to have to increase my efforts in maintaining my health.

Any athlete fine-tunes his body and maintains his fitness through a rigorous training regimen. If he doesn't, his abilities will decline and the competition will soon leave him far behind. Though you may not be an athlete, you are running the race of life. And as you run, you are dependent upon your body and responsible to care for it. If you are going to run to win, you need to guard your health.

TWICE-OWNED

In the previous chapter, we learned about financial stewardship. Your money is owned by God and distributed to you as his representative. He calls you to faithfully steward it. As the owner, God has the right to your money, and as the steward, you hold the responsibility for your money. In effect, the same is true of your body. Your body is also owned by God. In fact, if you are a Christian, your body is twice-owned by God.

God owns your body as its creator. He hand-crafted every bit of your DNA. David celebrates God's good design in Psalm 139, where he says, "For you formed my inward parts; you knitted me together in my mother's womb. I praise you, for I am fearfully and wonderfully made. Wonderful are your works; my soul knows it very well" (13–14). David's body was actually God's possession, carefully designed and deliberately assigned. The same is true for you—God owns your body because he created your body.

God owns your body as its Savior. You had rebelled against God and sinfully claimed your body as your own. You decided to negate God's claim over your body and to assert ownership of it yourself. But God drew you back from this treasonous rebellion, and as you accepted his offer of forgiveness and reconciliation, you ceded all your rights and restored proper ownership. In return, God actually took up residence within. So Paul asks, "Do you not know that your body is a temple of the Holy Spirit within you, whom you have from God? You are not your own, for you were bought with a price. So glorify God in your body" (1 Corinthians 6:19–20). This is why he can appeal to you and every other Christian "to present your bodies as a living sacrifice, holy and acceptable to God, which is your spiritual worship" (Romans 12:1). To present your body as a living sacrifice is to present everything you have and everything you are to his service, to place it all under his authority.

Your body is not your own. Your body is God's, to be cared for as he demands, to be committed to his service.

WHAT GOD EXPECTS

What does God, the owner of your body, expect from you as its steward? He expects that you will *present* it, *steward* it, *nurture* it, and *employ* it.

You need to present your body. You are a whole person, your body and soul knit carefully together. As we saw in Romans 12, you are to surrender to God all that you are, holding nothing back. Your body belongs to God and is to be used for his purposes. Thus, God calls you to surrender your body to him, to dedicate it to his service, to commit it to his purposes.

You need to steward your body. As you surrender your body, you acknowledge that it does not belong to you but to God. Just as you are responsible to faithfully steward your time and money, you are responsible before God to faithfully steward the body he has assigned to you. You are to use your body wisely, to put your body to use in ways that bring glory to God. After all, as we have seen, "You are not your own, for you were bought with a price. So glorify God in your body" (1 Corinthians 6:19–20).

You need to nurture your body. There is an inseparable unity between body, mind, and soul. When you neglect your body, you will often find your soul heavy and your mind dark. But when you care for it, you tend to find your soul cheerful and your mind enlightened. You can see some of this in John's prayer for his friend Gaius: "Beloved, I pray that all may go well with you and that you may be in good health, as it goes well with your soul" (3 John 2). For Gaius to be as active and effective as possible in God's work, he must have a healthy body and a healthy soul. If you wish to tend to your soul and mind, you must nurture your body. To honor God in all that you are, you must eat well, exercise frequently, and rest regularly.

You need to employ your body. Inner godliness is to be displayed in outward acts of kindness. James shows the unity of faith and works in this illustration: "If a brother or sister is poorly clothed and lacking in daily food, and one of you says to them, 'Go in peace, be warmed and filled,' without giving them the things needed for the body, what good is that? So also faith by itself, if it does not have works, is dead" (James 2:15–17). The love of God in your heart is to be displayed by the works of your hands. Young men are at their physical peak and bear a double responsibility to use that strength for the good of others. "The glory of young men is their strength," says Solomon, "but the splendor of old men is their gray hair" (Proverbs 20:29).

Many people today hold to a form of the ancient heresy of gnosticism. They believe the soul has great significance while the body is merely a useless vessel to be used or abused. But as Christians we see that people, made in the image of God, have much greater unity than this. To care for the body is to care for the soul.

DO IT NOW

With that in mind, let's consider how you can begin right now to guard your health.

- *Plan to be fit.* Paul warns that "while bodily training is of some value, godliness is of value in every way, as it holds promise for the present life and also for the life to come" (1 Timothy 4:8). This is a warning about neglecting spiritual fitness in favor of physical fitness. But it does not diminish the importance of being fit, for Paul still acknowledges it "is of some value." While we know that physical strength is fleeting, that it peaks early and goes into long decline, we also know that our bodies, minds, and spirits operate better in a fit body than an unfit one. Plan to get fit and stay fit through wise, moderate eating and regular, vigorous exercise.

- *Guard against idleness.* In another chapter we have discussed the plague and captivity of idleness. Even a quick study of the biblical teaching on the subject will show that much of our unhealthy living is a result of idleness, of the refusal to prioritize our bodies. Guard against the idleness that keeps you on the couch when you should be active.

- *Guard against gluttony.* Very little is said about the sin of gluttony in our day. Many Christians rightly strive to guard themselves against pride, lust, and greed, while failing to address their lack of self-control toward food. If you find yourself constantly drawn to the pantry and fridge, if you find yourself always needing to load up at the dessert table, it may say more about you than you think. As Jerry Bridges writes, "The person who overindulges his body at this point will find it more and more difficult to mortify other sinful deeds of the body. The habit of always giving in to the desire for food or drink will extend to other areas."[3] Food is a great gift, but it makes a terrible god. Learn to practice self-control toward food and renounce any sign of gluttony.

- *Prepare for the decline.* Strength peaks early and declines for many, many years. As your body and perhaps even your mind grows weak, there will be many new temptations to sin. Read Ecclesiastes 12:1–8 as a glimpse of your own biography and ask, "What will sustain me in that day?" The answer is simple: godly character. Nothing but godly character will sustain you as your body decays and your mind weakens. Even while you give attention to your physical health, do not neglect your spiritual well-being.

RUN TO WIN!

There is a close connection between physical fitness and spiritual fitness. In fact, there is a close connection between physical health and every other kind of health—mental, emotional, relational, and so on. When your body is unhealthy, and especially unhealthy through neglect, the rest of you is unlikely to be fit and sharp. Make it a priority to care for the body God has given you. Know that if you are going to run to win, you must guard your health.

STRENGTH FOR THE RACE

Notice that two of the key verses mentioned in this chapter make a point of saying that the reason for guarding our health is the gracious promises of the gospel: Romans 12:1 says "by the mercies of God" and 1 Corinthians 6:20 adds "you were bought with a price." We don't present our bodies as a living sacrifice in an attempt to earn our salvation, and we aren't trying to cause God to love us by glorifying him in our bodies. We should present our bodies to God because he has already given us mercies beyond measure, and we should glorify Christ because he has already bought us with his own precious blood. When you are tempted to give up (or not even start) because it seems impossible for your health to improve, or it will take so long for your body to get in shape, remember that the Lord loves and blesses you based on the righteousness of Christ, not the quality of your performance. One of his mercies to us, as a result of his sacrifice on our behalf, is the promise that "all things work together for good [even bad health], for those who are called according to his purpose" (Romans 8:28).

12

CONTROL YOUR SEXUALITY

This book had its genesis in a number of real-world conversations. In one of them (held in an appropriate context), a woman told of her struggles with her husband. She considered herself a caring and attentive wife who for many years had done her best to respond to her husband's frequent requests for sex. Yet even when she responded positively, she found his desire was rarely quenched, and within hours he would be after her again, grumbling and dissatisfied if she declined. Another young wife learned that her husband was regularly masturbating when she wasn't around. *Do all men do this?*, she wondered. Still another found a trail of pornography on her husband's laptop. *Is this normal? If so, why does it feel so wrong?*

It feels so wrong because it *is* so wrong. It isn't normal, and it isn't okay. As I pondered these situations, I asked myself, *What do these men really need?* Surely their inability and unwillingness to control their sexuality reveals a much deeper spiritual problem. I pondered and plotted. And now I want to challenge you in this way: If you are going to run to win, you need to control your sexuality.

AN AGE OF INCONTINENCE

I suppose we all know what it is to be incontinent. I was once in an airplane with a passenger who struggled in this way, and in a sealed aluminum tube soaring at 30,000 feet, her problem quickly became our problem. When we speak of continence we are usually referring to bodily functions, especially the ability or inability to control urinary and fecal functions. But the word has a wider meaning than that. In reading older Christian authors, you will often encounter the notion of continence applied to sexuality. A man who exercises sexual self-control is a continent man. Conversely, a man who lacks sexual self-control is an incontinent man, and far more harmful to himself and others than the one who cannot or will not control his bowels.

Sexual incontinence dominates the world today. Sexual expression and carnal pleasure are regarded as unassailable rights. Children not even old enough to understand their bodies are encouraged to explore, for masturbation is said to be physically pleasurable and morally commendable. From a young age, children are taught that anything consensual must be ethical and that repressing sexual desire is far more harmful than expressing it. Teens are told that abstinence is old-fashioned and that any sexual expression is fair game as long as they use protection. Sex: our bodies long for it, society celebrates it, pop culture promotes it, pornography trains us in it.

Sadly, sexual incontinence pervades the church as well. Many men who profess faith in Jesus Christ are out of control in their sexuality. Perhaps they developed bad habits when they were young and have simply never replaced those habits with better ones. Perhaps they've let themselves slip and over time have allowed healthy patterns to be displaced by unhealthy ones. Perhaps they are simply apathetic about the whole thing. Either way, we see the brutal fallout in churches ruined, ministries undermined, families wrecked. Many men have been willing to risk it all for the sake of fleeting sexual pleasure.

No wonder, then, that the Bible calls Christian men to self-control in all of life in general, and in this area in particular. To men struggling with sexual self-control, God's Word offers stern rebukes and sweet promises of forgiveness and reformed behavior. The very gospel that saves your soul is the gospel that grants the virtue of self-control.

A MAN OF SELF-CONTROL

Self-control is a virtue of uncommon beauty, the promised result of a relationship with God, for "the fruit of the Spirit is love, joy, peace, patience, kindness, goodness, faithfulness, gentleness, self-control" (Galatians 5:22–23). Yet it is a rare virtue because so few Christians diligently seek it. In the morass of a sinful mind, self-control can feel like captivity, the denial of what is good and satisfying. In reality, though, self-control is the key to what is good and satisfying, for it steers you away from counterfeits and directs you toward the greatest sources of the highest pleasures.

God is the creator of the gift of sexuality and, as its creator, the one who has defined its purpose and determined its boundaries. The greatest enjoyment of the gift is found within God's boundaries, not outside of them. Paul speaks to you when he appeals to the Christians in Rome "to present your bodies as a living sacrifice, holy and acceptable to God, which is your spiritual worship" (Romans 12:1). Their presentation of their bodies was their surrender of their very selves. You, too, must voluntarily surrender everything to God, including your sexuality. You must determine to seek his purposes for it and use it only in ways he permits.

God says that sex is given to a husband and wife for pleasure and procreation, a gift through which they enjoy unique intimacy and create new people formed in God's image. With this in mind, God gives you sexual desires so that you will pursue a wife first, and then so that you will pursue your wife within marriage. And, as you already know, God tends to give men a greater measure of sexual desire, perhaps to encourage the man to take the lead in the loving pursuit of his bride. We are, after all, prone to laziness and shirking our responsibilities. Perhaps God has given us this increased sexual desire to motivate us to do what we would otherwise avoid or procrastinate about.

According to the Designer, sex is a good gift that is inextricably tied to the marriage covenant. It is only within marriage that you are called to voluntarily give the rights over your body to your spouse. Paul explains it in this way: "For the wife does not have authority over her own body, but the husband does. Likewise the husband does not have authority over his own body, but the wife does" (1 Corinthians 7:4). Any and all sexual activity is to be enjoyed consensually between a husband and wife. You have no right to pursue sexual activity on your own. Your sexuality belongs to your wife, and only she can determine when and how it is expressed. This means you have no right to ogle other women, to concoct inappropriate fantasies, to stare at pornographic images, or to sneak off and masturbate. In all ways and at all times you are to show self-control, to withhold sexual expression for any purpose other than making love to your wife.

It is possible that your wife will not desire sex as often as you do. It is probable that there will be extended periods when, for various reasons, she will not able to participate at all or as freely as the two of you might like. In these times you will have the choice to sin or show self-control. Too many men choose sin! Too many sin by badgering their wives, by wallowing in self-pity, or by engaging in secret sexual sin. Some go so far as to force themselves on their wives, to make a horrific mockery of God's gift by brutally seizing what is meant to be gently won and lovingly received. The antidote to it all is self-control, that precious virtue that keeps the good gift within its proper boundaries.

My friend, if God has granted you a wife, he has also granted you the joy of pursuing her, of enjoying her, and of finding pleasure in her. This is the only context in which he endorses sexual activity of any kind. If God has not granted you a wife, he has called you to refrain from all sexual activity.

As a single man, you may not yet experience the pleasure of sex, but you can experience the pleasure of obedience. Even Jesus, the one who shows the way to be most fully human, lived and died a virgin. There is pleasure in sex, but much greater pleasure in obedience.

DO IT NOW

All of this calls for action. Here are a few places to begin.

- *Stop masturbating.* Is that too blunt? I don't think it is. I think men need to hear it. Whether you're single or married, just stop. Masturbation is self-love. It runs entirely counter to the heart of our Savior, who "came not to be served but to serve" (Mark 10:45). It is counterfeit and fraudulent sexuality. Because it involves no woman, it is actually closer to homosexuality than heterosexuality. It's immature, it's a misuse of God's gift, it's just plain dumb. You ought to be ashamed and embarrassed by it. So cut it out already and show some self-control.

- *Bounce your heart, not just your eyes.* I am sure you are well familiar with the temptation to allow your eyes to linger on the female form. I am almost equally sure you have been given the common advice to "bounce your eyes." It is well and good to stop looking at what is not yours to have, but do better than that—bounce your heart. The Bible assures us that evil does not begin with our eyes but with our hearts. The heart, after all, is the seat of our deepest desires and affections. As you address the behavior of your eyes, do not neglect to reform the desires of your heart.

- *Get accountability.* As men we tend to harbor our thoughts, to bury our questions, concerns, and secrets. Yet there is joy and freedom in unburdening ourselves, to externalizing what we prefer to internalize. Find a good friend, perhaps one who is older and wiser than you, and speak openly and freely about your sexual sin and victories. Ask that friend to hold you accountable and to help train you in godliness. "Confess your sins to one another and pray for one another, that you may be healed. The prayer of a righteous person has great power as it is working" (James 5:16).

- *Give it all.* Make the commitment to surrender 100 percent of your sexuality to God and to direct 100 percent of your sexual energy to your wife. Pursue her with gentleness and love. When she refuses you, respond with grace. When she accepts you, respond with joy. Enjoy her. Enjoy all of her for as long as you both shall live.

- *Seek and receive forgiveness.* When Paul wrote to the church in Corinth he recounted some of the sexual sin they had once participated in, but reminded them that they had since been recreated: "And such were some of you. But you were washed, you were sanctified, you were justified in the name of the Lord Jesus Christ and by the Spirit of our God" (1 Corinthians 6:11). If you are in Christ, this is true of you. Your sexual sin of the past—whether decades ago or hours ago—has been forgiven by Jesus Christ. Seek his forgiveness, receive it, then live as one from whom the power of sin has been broken. You can be free.

RUN TO WIN!

The Bible commands and commends sexual self-control. Yet there is one way in which it promotes and celebrates indulgence. Writing to young men, Solomon warns of the danger of illicit sexuality and wanton women, then says this: "Rejoice in the wife of your youth, a lovely deer, a graceful doe. Let her breasts fill you at all times with delight; be intoxicated always in her love" (Proverbs 5:19). Go ahead and get intoxicated, he says, but get drunk in the love and passionate pursuit of your wife. What wine does to your body, let your wife do to your affections and desires. Let her captivate you. Let her fascinate you. Let her have that kind of power over you. Be addicted to her. When you are with her, when you are in her arms, let yourself go and enjoy God's good gift of sexual pleasure. As you run to win, enjoy the wife God gives you, and control your sexuality.

STRENGTH FOR THE RACE

The gospel promises us freedom from the penalty and power of sin, and that includes sexual sin. You don't have to give up the fight or wallow in despair because of your failures, and you really *can* change even long-time habits by the power of the Holy Spirit. "Where sin increased, grace abounded all the more" (Romans 5:20) and God's grace is greater than all our sin—that is a necessary and sufficient source of strength for us in this very difficult part of our lives. When Peter tells husbands to "live with your wives in an understanding way," he adds, "since they are heirs with you of the grace of life" (1 Peter 3:7). And the commands to love and cherish our wives in Ephesians 5:25–30 flow grammatically from the command to "be filled with the Spirit" in Ephesians 5:18 (the passages that follow verse 18 are explanations of what it means to be filled with the Spirit in our relationships). So whether we succeed or fail, we should always ask God for his grace to forgive and empower us, for his Spirit to guide and provide—and we should rely on him alone for the help and hope we need.

13

CONSIDER YOUR LEGACY

There is something almost absurd about inheritances in a world of financial abundance and increased lifespans. Many in the Baby Boomer generation have worked hard and saved diligently, stuffing away untold billions in savings and retirement accounts, with the hope of leaving their children in a comfortable financial position. Meanwhile, in the West, lifespans are increasing, and many of those Boomers will live long into their 80s and 90s. By the time they die, their children will be grown and well-established in life. Whatever inheritance the parents pass along may well be superfluous by that time. Their children may well simply stuff that cash into their own bank accounts and leave it untouched until it is passed to yet another generation who likely will also have little use for it. Inheritances that were once necessary to establish and provide are now increasingly redundant.

This doesn't mean that what we leave behind is useless. The Bible has a lot to say about inheritances, about the legacy one generation leaves to the next. It commends hard work and diligent saving. It praises the man who passes something along to his children and grandchildren. But it also reminds us there is something you can leave behind that is of much greater significance than money. My friend, you are running the race of life, and if you are going to run to win, you need to consider your legacy.

MORE THAN MONEY

Christian financial planners are fond of quoting a particular proverb: "A good man leaves an inheritance to his children's children, but the sinner's wealth is laid up for the righteous" (Proverbs 13:22). You do not need a degree in Bible interpretation to understand the point of the proverb: it is good for a man to think ahead and to live in such a way that he provides not only for himself but also for his descendants. Many contemporary authors take this verse as a mandate for financial saving and estate planning. Yet before we apply the proverb to our own lives and times, we need to set it in its context.

In ancient Israel, land was sacred, for God had assured his covenant people that they would possess the promised land. Owning much land was a sign of God's blessing while owning no land was a sign of God's disfavor. Thus, land had unique significance. Not only that, but Israelites were largely subsistence farmers. Without land, they would soon starve, become dependent upon charity, or even be enslaved. A diligent father bore the responsibility of maintaining his land and passing it to the next generation.

That context is very different from our own. Since that time, Jesus Christ was born into the world. He lived and died and was raised, and as he did so, he fulfilled God's promises. He fulfilled the promise of a particular people inheriting a promised land. Ownership of land no longer indicates God's blessing or disfavor, since Jesus himself had "nowhere to lay his head" (Matthew 8:20). Besides this, the world has advanced and few of us are subsistence farmers who commit our lives to tending the family homestead. Land and inheritances have much less significance than they once did.

While we must be careful about the manner in which we apply this proverb to our times, we must be equally careful to heed its wisdom and consider our legacies. There is wisdom in looking to the future and determining how we would like to be remembered. There is value in considering the legacy we will leave to those who follow us. What we aim to leave behind after we die sets the course for how we intend to live.

So what legacy do you wish to leave to your children and to future generations? What inheritance would you like them to receive? Have you considered your legacy?

A BETTER INHERITANCE

The New Testament continues to speak of inheritances, but in a much different way. In Peter's first letter, he praises God for the inheritance bequeathed to us. This is not a financial or physical inheritance, but something far greater.

Blessed be the God and Father of our Lord Jesus

Christ! According to his great mercy, he has caused us to be born again to a living hope through the resurrection of Jesus Christ from the dead, to *an inheritance that is imperishable, undefiled, and unfading*, kept in heaven for you, who by God's power are being guarded through faith for a salvation ready to be revealed in the last time. (1 Peter 1:3–5)

Like a good father, God planned far in advance what he would leave to his children, and he worked diligently to obtain it. Through the life, death, and resurrection of Jesus Christ, he has provided the gifts of salvation, sanctification, and glorification. He has made us heirs of God and co-heirs with Christ. Ultimately, he has given us himself. Our greatest inheritance is God—peace with God, relationship with God, eternity with God. This inheritance has been granted, set aside, and is being kept safely as we wait for the day we can fully possess it. Paul tells us that we have been "sealed with the promised Holy Spirit, *who is the guarantee of our inheritance* until we acquire possession of it, to the praise of his glory" (Ephesians 1:13–14). We have begun to receive what God has set aside for us, but we will receive it fully and finally only in God's eternal kingdom.

Like God, you are responsible to plan far in advance what you will leave your children, and you, too, should work diligently to obtain it. God expects you to leave your children an inheritance. But he expects more than that. He also expects you to consider your spiritual family, the church, and determine what inheritance you would like to leave to them. This inheritance, this legacy, may include finances, but it must include treasures far more valuable than that. Here is how J.R. Miller says it:

> If parents give money to their children, they may lose it in some of life's vicissitudes. If they bequeath to them a home of splendor, they may be driven out of it. If they pass down to them as a heritage an honored name, they may sully it. But if they fill their hearts with the holy influences and memories of a happy Christian home, no calamity, no great sorrow, no power of evil, no earthly loss, can ever rob them of their sacred possessions.[4]

Your first legacy is the gospel. If you leave your children full pockets but empty souls, you have neglected your most important duty. Of course, you cannot force your children to turn to Christ. But you can teach them the gospel and plead with them to accept it. God calls you to diligently teach and train them "in the discipline and instruction of the Lord" (Ephesians 6:4) and to trust that as you do so, they will respond to the gospel by putting their faith in Jesus Christ. And you are to share this same gospel with friends, neighbors, colleagues, and whoever else will listen. There is nothing in the world more precious than souls and no greater legacy than souls won for Christ.

Your second legacy is godliness. Paul celebrated this kind of legacy in his friend Timothy's background when he said, "I am reminded of your sincere faith, a faith that dwelt first in your grandmother Lois and your mother Eunice and now, I am sure, dwells in you as well" (2 Timothy 1:5). Timothy had received the legacy of a sincere godliness from both his mother and grandmother. As Timothy grew up, he encountered Paul who related to him as a father to a son, even referring to him as "my true child in the faith" (1 Timothy 1:2). Paul meant to leave him a similar legacy: "You, however, have followed my teaching, my conduct, my aim in life, my faith, my patience, my love, my steadfastness, my persecutions and sufferings" (2 Timothy 3:10–11). He would say to Timothy, in effect, as to so many others, "Follow my example" (2 Timothy 1:13) or "Imitate me" (1 Corinthians 4:16; Philippians 3:17; 2 Thessalonians 3:7). Paul pursued godly character so he could call Timothy and others to follow his example.

There is much else you can leave behind. You can leave possessions, businesses, land, or money. Well and good. But nothing is more precious, more valuable, or more praiseworthy than a legacy of gospel and godliness.

DO IT NOW

Let's consider a few practical steps you can take beginning right now.

- *Plan for your legacy.* What legacy would you like to leave? Having considered this, begin to plan how you will accomplish that. The man who wants to leave his children a million dollars must plan to generate and save enough income to reach his goal; the man who wants to leave his children a legacy of godliness must plan how he will grow in godliness and share the gospel.

- *Assess your life.* Get an accurate assessment of whether your life is in line with the legacy you want to leave. Think about the last job you left or the last place you moved from: What kind of legacy did you leave there? Do people miss your presence, or was your departure good riddance? It's likely that the legacies you leave now will be similar to the ultimate legacy you leave when you die. Ask those closest to you for honest feedback: What comes to their mind when they think of you? Do your wife and children and closest friends think of godly traits or worldly traits? For better or for worse, the life you're living now determines the legacy you'll leave later.

- *Go to the cross.* Because of the cross of Christ, there is no sin that cannot be washed and there is no legacy that cannot be redeemed. Saul of Tarsus was widely known as a persecutor of Christians. But because of Christ's intervention, he became known as the one who is "now preaching the faith he once tried to destroy" (Galatians 1:23). While you have breath, you still have time to change your legacy. It all begins with receiving forgiveness from Christ. It begins with admitting before Christ that your sin has ruined your legacy and trusting that he has the power to transform you. And once you've received his forgiveness, you can put off the old self with its ruined legacy and put on the new self, who is growing into godliness and depositing the gospel to others.

- *Work hard now.* Every day, with each passing minute, with every tiny decision, you are forming your legacy. It's not the grand moments of life but rather unremarkable, unnoticed persistence that forms a legacy. Your detailed plans and good intentions will do no good if you don't follow them with action. If you want to leave a godly legacy, get started now. Don't waste another moment. Give yourself to eternal investments that will leave the greatest legacy for your children.

RUN TO WIN!

I think I speak for multitudes when I say I don't care a lick whether my parents leave me as much as a penny of inheritance. They have already given me a far more important and enduring inheritance. They introduced me to the gospel and rejoiced as I put my faith in Christ. They modeled godliness, setting an example of how I was to live as a Christian. Is that the inheritance you intend to leave your children? Are you working toward it? If you are going to run to win, you must consider your legacy.

STRENGTH FOR THE RACE

The heavenly inheritance we have received from our gracious God is a source of motivation and power for us to leave a legacy here. And it is a great source of hope: in addition to the fact that in this life it's never too late to be forgiven for your failures and change your legacy to a positive one (like the thief on the cross, for example), we also know that God's loving Providence is able to take even the bad things we've done and use them for good in the lives of those we care about (Romans 8:28). They can learn from our mistakes, of course, and they can be impacted by how we repent and make restitution for them. All of this is sufficient reason to keep picking ourselves up, by the grace of God, and persevere in running the race for the sake of generations yet to come.

PART 3

DISCIPLINES
OF RELATIONSHIP

14

FOSTER YOUR FRIENDSHIPS

Charles Spurgeon said that "the voices of childhood echo through life" in such a way that the "first learned is generally the last forgotten." The lessons we learn in our earliest years tend to remain fixed to the end. This is tremendously beneficial when the lessons have been sound, but terribly detrimental when they have not. One harmful lesson men often learn early in life is that they should be suspicious of relationships with other men.

From our youngest days we are taught that friendship can only be so close before our closeness threatens to "out" us. When a friendship looks too friendly we may be called "Sissy!" at best, or "Queer!" at worst. We are expected to play rough and tumble games together, to compete, and to poke fun at one another. But we have to be wary of relational closeness or dependency, because the other boys are watching with suspicion and judgment. We don't want to be seen as needy or emotional. Parents may even be watching uneasily, wondering if relational intimacy may portend weakness, femininity, or even sexual desire. Men are to be strong, independent, and self-reliant. We can have pals, we can be buddies, but we must not love one another.

In this book we have been looking at a number of issues related to godly manhood. Employing the great metaphor of life as a race, we have seen that men who run their race victoriously apply themselves to a variety of important disciplines. We have seen that some of these are related to faith and some are related to life. In the final five chapters we will turn to matters of relationship, including your wife, your children, and your local church. But first, we will consider your friends. If you are going to run to win, you must foster good friendships.

THE BOOK OF FRIENDSHIP

The Bible has a lot to say about friendship. We could even argue that friendship is one of the Bible's major themes—the Bible is the Book of Friendship!

God existed from all eternity in the friendship of the Trinity, with Father, Son, and Holy Spirit enjoying a perfect, unbroken relationship with one another. God created human beings to enter into that existing friendship, to enjoy what God already enjoyed in himself. Creator invited creature to participate in something beyond wonderful. Tragically, we rebelled against God and, through our betrayal, ruptured that friendship. We walked away and were content to exist on our own, severed from God.

But God is a good friend—the kind who initiates reconciliation even though he is the innocent party. To do this, he sent his Son, Jesus, into the world to be a friend to sinners, to defeat the sin that separated them and draw them back into relationship with the Father. And now, by putting our faith in Jesus Christ, we are restored to what we once enjoyed. Though we cannot now see God face to face, we wait with eager anticipation for the day Christ returns and restores to us all the intimacy we once experienced. We will be forever with God, forever his friends.

The friendship we experience with God provides the model for the friendships we can and should experience with other human beings. The intimacy God calls us to enjoy with others is not based merely on common interests or shared experiences. It looks beyond gender and color or any other easy division. It is a truly spiritual friendship in which we are bound together by God, in God, and for God. Because it is a spiritual friendship, it will exist beyond this earth and beyond the grave. It will endure forever.

THE MAN OF FRIENDSHIP

Friendship is a great gift of God. Spiritual friendship, friendship shared in Christ, is an even greater gift. Spiritual friendship with other godly men is one of life's greatest privileges and highest joys. Do you have a close friend? Are you a close friend to another man?

You need friends for the sake of your well-being. In recent years some revisionist biblical commentators have looked with suspicion on the relationship of David and Jonathan. Some have read David's lament upon Jonathan's death and imagined them as a secretly gay couple: "I am distressed for you, my brother Jonathan; very pleasant have you been to me; your love to me was extraordinary, surpassing the love of women" (2 Samuel 1:26). But David is not weeping for a lover who shared his bed, but a friend who shared his life. Proverbs 17:17 says, "A friend loves at all times, and a brother is born for adversity." Through the turmoil of constant betrayal, multiple marriages, and running for his life, David could always count on his friend Jonathan. Theirs was the truest and deepest kind of friendship that endured every form of adversity. Do you have friends who love you at all times and are at your side during hardships?

You also need spiritual friendships for the sake of your soul. You are a sinful person who can hold tight to your depravity. You are a weak-eyed person who often cannot see yourself as you are. You are a selfish person who sometimes struggles to live for anyone or anything apart from yourself. You need friends who will help you, serve you, strengthen you, equip you. You need friends to temper your weakness, to challenge your sinfulness, to comfort your sorrows, to speak truth into your tragedies. "Iron sharpens iron," says Solomon, "and one man sharpens another" (Proverbs 27:17). Who sharpens you? Who is sharpened by you?

Truly, friendships are a great gift from a great God. Theologian Hugh Black says,

Friends should be chosen by a higher principle of selection than any worldly one. They should be chosen for character, for goodness, for truth and trustworthiness, because they have sympathy with us in our best thoughts and holiest aspirations, because they have community of mind in the things of the soul. All other connections are fleeting and imperfect.[5]

DO IT NOW

Having looked at the beauty and necessity of friendships, let's consider some ways to practically apply this in our lives.

- *Examine your friendships.* Not all friendships are helpful because not all friendships are truly spiritual. Wise old Solomon commends good friends and warns against foolish friends when he says, "Whoever walks with the wise becomes wise, but the companion of fools will suffer harm" (Proverbs 13:20). This does not mean that we cannot enjoy friendships with non-Christians. But many Christian men spend all of their time with those who don't know Christ, robbing their own soul of the benefits of a spiritual friendship. Examine your friendships to ensure you have friends who are wise and that you are not spending inordinate amounts of time with fools. While you may be able to influence them for good, it is just as likely they will influence you for evil.

- *Pray for friendships.* Ask God to grant you friendships. This is a good and noble request to make of the God who is your friend.

- *Find a friend.* The main factor that keeps us from friendship is our pride. We are ashamed to initiate friendships, afraid to look desperate or pathetic as we ask another man for some of his time. Don't be dumb. Don't deny yourself something so good simply because you are too proud to seek it. Many men are just like you—wanting and needing a friend, yet too proud to ask. Man up and go find a friend.

- *Be a good friend.* A friendship, like any other relationship, requires effort—effort that is usually measured in time. Friendships thrive when they are given sufficient time and wither when they are not. Consider opportunities for face-to-face time (sitting together over coffee or another beverage) and side-by-side time (working together on a project or enjoying a hobby or activity together). Your relationship will grow in different ways in each context.

RUN TO WIN!

Of all the gifts God gives, few are more precious than friendship, an enduring, sacrificial commitment to another person. Yet of all the gifts God gives to men, few are more likely to be overlooked than this one. Still, the Bible assures us: "A man of many companions may come to ruin, but there is a friend who sticks closer than a brother" (Proverbs 18:24). Find that man in someone else, and be that man to him. If you are going to run to win, you need to foster your friendships.

STRENGTH FOR THE RACE

The hesitations many men have about developing close friendships are a very real impediment, especially if we have been burned or betrayed by one or more close friends during our lifetimes. But we need to get our focus off ourselves and onto meeting the needs of others. Think about the words of the old hymn, "What a Friend We Have in Jesus." He sought out friendship with us even though we were his enemies (Romans 5:10), and he remains our friend even though we have not been a good friend to him in many ways. And he provides an example for how we can developer healthy relationships with others. Like the song says, friendship starts with caring, asking questions, and then listening ("all our sins and griefs to bear; what a privilege to carry everything to God in prayer"). Jesus cares about what is going on in our lives, so we should show that same concern for others, and when we do he will supply the right kind and number of relationships that will meet our own needs in return.

15

ACCEPT YOUR LEADERSHIP

Some facets of life in our modern world are made more difficult than they really need to be. They have been debated and written about to such a degree that they've become almost impossibly complicated. I'm convinced that one such area is leadership, and especially leadership in the home and family. What should be clear has become woefully muddied.

Meanwhile, our world is crying out for leadership—good leadership, confident leadership, humble leadership, the kind of leadership that uses authority to bless rather than curse, to give rather than take. If you are a husband or a father, you are called to that kind of leadership. Husband, God calls you to lead your wife. Dad, God calls you to lead your children. As we consider together what it means to live a life that honors God, we come to an indispensable truth: If you are going to run to win, you need to accept your leadership.

WHY MEN DON'T LEAD

Leadership is not easy. Leadership does not come naturally to many people, and truly biblical leadership does not come naturally to anyone. It is such a rare quality that few of us have been able to learn from godly examples. It is such a precious quality that we treasure the few examples we do have. Thankfully, God has given us all we need in his Word to learn how to lead.

Before we turn there to learn from God together, perhaps it is first worth considering why so many men do not lead their families. I suggest the following four reasons.

Ignorance. Some men simply do not understand that they are called to lead. They have not read the appropriate Bible passages or have never grappled with them enough to understand their implications. Many attend churches that have not faithfully taught their members that God calls men to accept and embrace their role as leaders in the home.

Uncertainty. Some men know what God calls them to, but they suffer from self-doubt. They wonder if and how they could ever be leaders. Some know their wives are smarter, godlier, more knowledgeable, or more mature than they are, and they allow these factors to keep them from embracing their role. Others have tried and met resistance, tried and given up, or tried and blown it. Their confidence is shot, and they live in a place of uncertainty.

Fear. Some men succumb to fear. They may be intimidated by the responsibility bound up in leadership or silenced by the many voices that disparage it. Leadership sometimes involves leading people who do not wish to be led and making unpopular decisions. Both can be scary! Equally scary are the voices around us mocking Christians for such old-fashioned notions as a division of roles within the family. Fear causes many men to back down from their God-given role.

Apathy. Some men are simply apathetic. They know they ought to lead but just don't care enough to do it. They know what the Bible says, they know the expectations upon them, but they find it too difficult or too demanding. So they sit back and do nothing at all.

HOW MEN SHOULD LEAD

Today we are drowning in books about leadership. Husbands, fathers, pastors, and employers have an endless catalog to consult if they wish to grow in their ability and confidence. At the same time, society is trending toward a kind of egalitarianism that disparages so many forms of leadership. It is a perplexing place to be. Yet, as we'd expect, the Bible offers timeless clarity.

In his letter to the Ephesians, Paul addresses both husbands and wives and does so, at least in part, to ensure each understands the unique role God has given them. To wives he says, "Wives, submit to your own husbands, as to the Lord. For the husband is the head of the wife even as Christ is the head of the church, his body, and is himself its Savior. Now as the church submits to Christ, so also wives should submit in everything to their husbands" (Ephesians 5:22–24). This affirms a pattern that God has built into the very structure of his creation—that husbands are to lead their families and that wives are to joyfully and willingly place themselves under their husband's leadership.

Since Paul has told wives to "submit to your own husbands," we would naturally assume that as he turns his attention to husbands he will tell them, "Husbands, lead your wives." But he doesn't. He assumes a husband will lead but is aware that without further instruction this leadership will be harsh, selfish, or inadequate. To counter this, he carefully defines the quality of a husband's leadership. Such leadership is to be gentle and tender, to imitate the love of Jesus Christ for his church. "Husbands, love your wives, as Christ loved the church and gave himself up for her.… In the same way husbands should love their wives as their own bodies. He who loves his wife loves himself" (Ephesians 5:25, 28)

In God's world, the roles of husbands and wives are complementary, not identical or interchangeable. Peter expresses it in similar terms: "Likewise, wives, be subject to your own husbands" and "Likewise, husbands, live with your wives in an understanding way" (1 Peter 3:1, 7). To the husband falls the role of leadership—leadership defined by gentleness, love, respect, and understanding. Of all we could say about leadership, this must remain preeminent: the foremost call in leadership is love. Christian leadership is not first charting vision or giving orders, but modeling and expressing godly character. Christian leadership is not concerned first with the leader but with the one being led. Ninety-nine percent of a husband's leadership is leadership in character. His call is to surge in holiness, to be obsessed with godliness, to stop at nothing to grow in righteousness. He is to be gentle toward his wife but brutal toward his sin. He is to treasure his bride but cast off his depravity. He ought to clearly demonstrate in his leadership that he loves his wife more than he loves himself.

And, of course, he is to behave in much the same way toward his children. After Paul has spoken to husbands and wives, he turns to children, then fathers. "Fathers, do not provoke your children to anger, but bring them up in the discipline and instruction of the Lord" (Ephesians 6:4). The fact that he speaks to fathers and not mothers emphasizes the man's leadership within the home, and perhaps also his tendency to ignore his responsibilities and defer child-raising to his wife. Yet God lays the responsibility on the father to be gentle with his children, to treat them with dignity, and to take responsibility for their spiritual growth.

There is so much more we could say. We could discuss the ins and outs of leadership. We could talk about providing vision, direction, and all of that. But instead, I want to call you once more to focus on character, because here's the thing: if you do well here, direction and decision-making will be far simpler. The husband who dwells in depravity will find that his family distrusts and resists his direction and decisions. Of course they will, because he's proven that in and of himself he is unsuited for leadership. But the husband who pursues holiness and grows in character will typically find that his family trusts him and joyfully embraces his decisions. Lead in character, and the rest will fall into place; fail to lead in character, and the rest will be chaos.

DO IT NOW

Here are some practical pointers on getting started in leading with love.

- *Prioritize devotion.* Be a man of the Word and a man of prayer. Nothing you do will so shape your family as your personal walk with God. Commit to reading the Bible and praying. Come up with a plan and follow it. Tell your family what you've been learning and share with them how you've been praying for them.

- *Lead family devotions.* With your personal devotional life in place, also lead your family in devotions. Find a time in the morning or evening where you can build a habit of gathering the family to read a short passage of the Bible and to pray together.

- *Lead your family to church.* Lead your family in their church attendance and commitment. Be the one who is most excited to be at church, the one who sings most fervently and listens most carefully. Be the one who speaks with your family afterward to ask what they've learned, and share how God worked in and through you.

- *Embrace your leadership.* Consider the four reasons I offered that men tend not to lead (ignorance, uncertainty, fear, and apathy) and whether any of them apply to you.

Repent of your failures to lead and determine that you will be the leader your wife and children need you to be.

RUN TO WIN!

Your family needs to be led. Your wife and children need you to be the leader God calls you to be. He calls you to lead in love, to study the life and character of Jesus Christ, and to imitate him. Do that and God will be pleased. Do that and your family will be blessed. Run to win by accepting and embracing your leadership.

STRENGTH FOR THE RACE

I mentioned earlier that some men try to lead and give up when they fail or otherwise become frustrated in their attempts. This is an all-too-common experience for Christian men. Perhaps they try to do it in their own strength without relying on the Spirit of God, or they do it in order to present themselves as a good man to others rather than doing it for the glory of God. If those are our motives, failure will be inevitable. And that is one of the biggest problems with a lot of leadership material today: it doesn't talk about the real source of our strength, which is the Holy Spirit, and the real purpose for our leadership, which is to glorify God. So I encourage you to spend some time in serious and honest prayer about what you are relying on in your leadership tasks, and the reasons you are doing them. Repent of any selfish or worldly motives and ask God to help you lead for his glory and the good of others.

16

TREASURE YOUR MARRIAGE

I won't ever forget the day I married Aileen. I won't ever forget the moment she appeared at the end of the aisle and began her slow walk toward me. Our eyes met, and in an instant I was overwhelmed with awe, overcome with the joy of being joined together for life. It was a holy, intense, unforgettable moment. My love was fierce and strong, and I was convinced there was nothing I wouldn't do for her, no trial I wouldn't endure on her behalf. By the time her father put her hand in mind, I was little more than a messy puddle of tears and snot (which rather dampened the sweetness of the moment, I think; I should have thought to put a handkerchief in my pocket.).

But sadly, it didn't take long for that kind of adoration to be replaced by impatience and immature squabbling. We hadn't been married for long when apathy began to replace fervor, when the highs began to give way to the inevitable mids and lows. The drama of the wedding day turned to normal life with all its stresses and trials and mundane moments. I soon learned that marriage is tougher than it seems. I soon learned that I'm more sinful than I had imagined.

For all that, our marriage has been good. Neither of us has ever been tempted to stray or to walk away. We've never fallen out of love or grown tired of spending time together. We were best friends before we were married and have remained that way ever since. There's no one I'd rather spend time with and no one with whom I share so many interests. Yet my great challenge from then until now has been treasuring my marriage. And I suspect this is your challenge as well. As we continue this book on being a godly man, we need to consider this: If you are going to run to win, you must treasure your marriage.

THE MEANING OF MARRIAGE

We are selfish people who are experts at identifying and doing those things that benefit ourselves. We can even misuse something as good as marriage, to see it as an institution that exists ultimately for our comfort, for our happiness, for our pleasure. And while marriage does bring all of those benefits and many more, it ultimately exists for something far better. Marriage exists to glorify God. Marriage exists to demonstrate the gospel.

Paul makes this link clear in Ephesians 5:32, where he calls marriage a "mystery" that refers to Christ and the church. What this tells us is that even before Christ lived and died for his people, the union of a husband and wife was a picture of what he would accomplish, a metaphor of the way he would love his people. We might even say God created marriage so we would have words and images through which we could learn about him. The sacrificial love of a husband for his wife would be a demonstration of Christ's love for his people. The wife's joyful response to her husband's pursuit would be a demonstration of the church's love of her Savior. The universal human institution of marriage was ultimately created by God for the purposes of God.

This cuts hard against the cultural ethos, which sees marriage as optional and perhaps even oppressive. It cuts hard against our inward selfishness, which would take all the benefits of marriage without the commitment. It elevates marriage to something far beyond itself. It makes marriage something holy, something to treasure.

TREASURING YOUR MARRIAGE

If God has given you a wife, he has given you a precious gift. He calls you to treasure your marriage, and to treasure marriage, you must treasure your bride. If you are to treasure your wife, you must learn from Jesus Christ how to love her well. Here are four marks of a husband's love. [6]

A sacrificial love. A husband's love is sacrificial. It sacrifices safety, comfort, desires, preferences or anything else if only it will serve her. Paul says, "Husbands, love your wives, as Christ loved the church and gave himself up for her." As a husband, you are to imitate Christ, who gave everything he had for the sake of his bride. I'm sure you know that you are called to love your wife to such a degree that you would be willing to die for her. Perhaps you have fantasized about going out in a blaze of glory as you save her from a fiery building or throwing her out of the way of a runaway train. But God calls for far more than this. God calls you to live for your wife, and this is a much greater challenge. This is a day-to-day, moment-to-moment calling to love and serve her. It is a call to study and know her so you can provide for her needs and submit to her desires. It is a call to put to death whatever sin you are clinging to that keeps you from loving her better and serving her deeper. Do you love your wife in a sacrificial way?

A purposeful love. Christ's love for his people accomplished something on their behalf—it accomplished their salvation. He "gave himself up for [the church], that he might sanctify her, having cleansed her by the washing of water with the word, so that he might present the church to himself in splendor, without spot or wrinkle or any such thing, that she might be holy and without blemish" (Ephesians 5:26). Christ died to both save and sanctify his people. As a husband, you are God's special means to help your wife grow in holiness. You are to imitate Jesus by helping your wife grow in holiness, to take upon yourself the solemn responsibility of applying God's Word to her life. Her spiritual maturity is your husbandly responsibility. You are responsible to know God's Word to such an extent that you can carefully and faithfully apply it to her. Do you love your wife in a purposeful way?

A nurturing love. The love of Christ is a gentle and

nurturing love, and it serves as the example of the kind of love a husband is to extend toward his wife. "In the same way husbands should love their wives as their own bodies. He who loves his wife loves himself. For no one ever hated his own flesh, but nourishes and cherishes it, just as Christ does the church, because we are members of his body" (Ephesians 5:28–30). To nourish your wife, you must consider how a gardener nourishes his plants, how he carefully draws out the beauty of each one. Richard Phillips says of the husband, "This requires him to pay attention to her, to talk with her in order to know what her hopes and fears are, what dreams she has for the future, where she feels vulnerable or ugly, and what makes her anxious or gives her joy." [7] To cherish your wife, you must treat her in ways that prove her value, that cause her to thrive. Do you love your wife in a nurturing way?

A steadfast love. The love of a husband is a steadfast, enduring kind of love. It expresses the highest commitment. "Therefore a man shall leave his father and mother and hold fast to his wife, and the two shall become one flesh" (Matthew 19:5). Just as Jesus Christ will never forsake his church, you as a husband must never forsake your wife. The permanence of the one-flesh union of marriage is sealed, signified, and repeatedly celebrated through sex. The permanence of the one-flesh union of marriage is mocked, undermined, and dishonored through adultery, pornography, and any other form of sexual sin. As a godly husband you vow to "forsake all others" not merely in deed, but also in thought, desire, and fantasy. Your wife thrives when she can count on the rock-solid assurance of your commitment to her; she withers in distrust and broken vows. Do you love your wife in a steadfast way?

The love you are meant to show your wife is sacrificial, purposeful, nurturing, and steadfast, just like the love of Christ for his church. It is in loving your wife this way that you treasure her, and it is in treasuring your wife that you treasure your marriage.

DO IT NOW

Treasuring your marriage requires action. Here are a few steps you can take right away.

- *Give your wife a voice.* It is wise to invite your wife to speak into your life. For this to happen well, you must allow her to speak freely, you must listen carefully, and you must respond only after careful reflection. It may be best to promise that you will not reply defensively for one hour or 24 hours or however long it takes you to prayerfully consider what she says. Perhaps ask, "How can I better serve you as your husband?" or "What is one sin you would love to see me address in my life?" or "What are some things I do that make you feel unloved, and what could I do instead?" Carve out some time, ask the questions, listen carefully, avoid prideful defensiveness, pray fervently, respond graciously.

- *Exclude all others.* When you married your wife, you committed yourself to her fully and completely. Yet many men allow room in their lives, their hearts, and their minds for other women. Allowing your mind to dwell on others will only ever cool your love and harm your relationship. There is no room in marriage for "what ifs" or "if onlys." Exclude any thoughts, desires, or fantasies for any other woman and commit yourself entirely to your bride.

- *Continue to pursue her.* It is tempting to see your wedding day as a kind of finish line. You pursued her, you wooed her, you won her, and now she's yours. But your wedding is not the finish line; it is the starting line. Continue to pursue her, to learn about her, to know her, to display your joy in her, to grow in your love toward her.

- *Continue to do love.* There will be times when your feelings of love will grow cool. But even though it may be difficult to feel love, there are always opportunities to *do* love. After all, love is more about action than emotion. Or as Sinclair Ferguson says it, "Love is not maximum emotion. Love is maximum commitment."[8] While you may at times lack romantic feelings, you'll never lack opportunities to do her good. Commit yourself to her good and always do those things that express love toward her, even and especially when you don't feel love.

RUN TO WIN!

I began this chapter with tears—the tears I experienced as my wife walked toward me on a sunny August morning in 1998.

I write this 19 years later and, as the chapter comes to a close, there are tears in my eyes once again. I am reminded of how often I've failed her. Having pondered the depth of Christ's love, I am aware of the shallowness of my own. Though I am the one who has written the chapter, I still have so much to learn, I still have so much room to grow. So this final charge goes to me, just as it does to you: If you are going to run to win, you must treasure your marriage.

STRENGTH FOR THE RACE

The principles we've discussed in this chapter from Ephesians 5:25–32 cannot be practiced rightly unless we are "filled with the Spirit" (Ephesians 5:18). Paul follows that first command with three adjectival participles, the last of which is "submitting to one another," and then adds explanations of how the Spirit enables us to relate properly to one another in the family and society. That grammatical connection tells us that the supernatural strength we need to love our wives like Christ loved the church can be traced back to the power of the Holy Spirit. All believers have been given the Spirit (Ephesians 1:13, 2:18, 3:16, 4:30), so all we need to do is allow him to "fill" or control us, and we can love like Christ loved. Colossians 3:16 mentions another source of strength when just before the command to love our wives, it says "let the word of Christ dwell in you richly." The truth of Scripture is "living and active" (Hebrews 4:12), so filling your heart and mind with it will remake you in the image of our Lord and make you more able to love like he does.

17

NURTURE YOUR CHILDREN

There are few roles in which we feel deeper inadequacy than our role as fathers. What suits us to the task of raising little people? What assurance can we have that we are doing it well? What will our children someday say of us? These are big and perplexing questions, so it is little wonder that church bulletin boards are covered with posters for parenting seminars and library shelves are groaning under the weight of parenting books. George Barna reported that in a recent 21-year period more than 75,000 books were published on the subject. Parenting is tough, and none of us is fully up to the challenge.

Considering the importance and difficulty of the task, we may find it surprising how little direct guidance the New Testament offers us. Its clearest instruction is found in Ephesians 6:4: "Fathers, do not provoke your children to anger, but bring them up in the discipline and instruction of the Lord." The parallel passage in Colossians 3:21 adds just one minor detail: "Fathers, do not provoke your children, lest they become discouraged." While we're grateful for this divine guidance, we are probably left wishing there was more of it. Couldn't God have answered a few more of our questions? What about spanking versus timeouts? What about homeschooling versus Christian or public schooling? What about the age to buy a child her first iPhone or the right way to oversee her selection of a spouse? Couldn't we have just a little bit more detail?

Yet as we carefully and prayerfully consider what God has given us, we see his wisdom. He may not have given us all we want, but he has lovingly provided all we need to be successful fathers. Before the Bible tells us how to parent, it first makes sure we understand why we parent. Once we understand the ultimate goal of parenting, then we see how these two short passages provide a wealth of insight on how to raise our children in godliness. If you are going to be a wise father, you must consider this: To run to win, you need to nurture your children.

WHY WE PARENT

What is the goal of our parenting? What is our key task? Is it to raise children who can function well in society? Is it to raise polite, well-educated, successful children? Is it to raise children who will accumulate great wealth or great accomplishments? According to the Bible, there is something of much greater importance. The key task of Christian parents is discipleship. As Chap Bettis says,

The foundational parenting text is not Ephesians 6:1–4 or Deuteronomy 6:4–9, as important as they are. Rather it is Matthew 28:18–20 ("Go therefore and make disciples of all nations, baptizing them in the name of the Father and of the Son and of the Holy Spirit, teaching them to observe all that I have commanded you. And behold, I am with you always, to the end of the age."). God's desire for your family is to be a Trinity-displaying, God-glorifying, disciple-making unit.[9]

Ultimately, your task as a parent is to nurture your children not first toward educational, financial, or vocational success, but toward Jesus Christ. Your primary role is that of the discipler. A key part of heeding God's commission to "make disciples of all nations" is to make disciples of your own children. What value is there in saving the whole world but neglecting your own children? The Great Commission begins in your own home with your own children.

Now, as we return to the instructions to parents in Ephesians and Colossians, we can put them in their proper context. These are words given to disciple-makers, to parents who are tasked with leading their children from darkness to light, from rebellion against God to joyful submission to him.

HOW NOT TO PARENT: DON'T PROVOKE OR DISCOURAGE

The wise father understands the power of his words and actions toward his children. With one harsh word, he can wound his daughter's heart. With one biting critique, he can discourage his son. While both of Paul's parallel passages contain the same exhortation ("Do not provoke"), Ephesians defines a specific kind of provocation: "Do not provoke your children to anger." "Provoke" is a word used to describe kindling a fire into flame—you begin with a tiny, glowing ember and provoke it into a mighty, roaring fire. Paul lays out a challenge: do not exasperate your children or irritate them in such a way that you provoke anger or bitterness, which will eventually lead to discouragement. The discouraged child is the one who has lost heart. He is hopeless and beaten down, he has lost motivation, he has stopped caring. Through arbitrary demands, through criticism never balanced with praise, through your own hypocritical living, and through so many other flaws of character, you can beat down a child to such an extent that he no longer cares to gain and maintain your approval.

Thus God exhorts you in this way: father, do not provoke your children to anger, lest they become discouraged. As fathers, we tend to blame our children's behavior on their own weaknesses and sinful tendencies. But in light of Paul's command, you must first ask yourself: in my parenting, have I provoked my children to anger or left them discouraged?

To provoke your children in this way represents a serious failure in parenting. But, of course, God does not leave you wondering how to avoid such a fate. He immediately follows with the solution: "But bring them up in the discipline and instruction of the Lord." Do not beat them down, but raise them up. Do not provoke them with impatience and injustice, but instead shepherd them with nurture and tenderness. The way you do this is with discipline and instruction.

HOW TO PARENT: DISCIPLINE AND INSTRUCT

The task of Christian parenting can be summed up in the words "discipline" and "instruction." Between them, they offer words that express both the negative and positive sides of the father's calling. At times you need to discipline your children, to correct them—sometimes with a look, sometimes with a word, sometimes with a timeout, and sometimes with a spank. The goal of discipline is not to display your displeasure with your children, nor is it to keep them from embarrassing you in the future. In light of the goal of parenting, discipline is meant to lovingly help your children see themselves as sinners before a holy God in need of a Savior. While I am sure you do not relish this part of your task, it is an inevitable aspect of being a father to sinful children. Indeed, it is a negative but necessary part of parenting.

Once we have properly disciplined our children, then we may introduce the positive side of parenting: instruction. Tedd

Tripp writes, "Properly administered discipline humbles the heart of a child, making him subject to parental instruction. An atmosphere is created in which instruction can be given."[10] To instruct your children, you must teach them, you must explain what is right, you must demonstrate how they are to live. And while it is good to teach them all kinds of knowledge and life skills, you must also teach them the deep spiritual truths that can save their souls. This is the positive side of parenting, the part you are meant to relish and enjoy.

In both discipline and instruction, you must remember that your primary task as a father is that of a discipler. Tripp writes, "What must you do in correction and discipline? You must require proper behavior. God's law demands that. You cannot, however, be satisfied to leave the matter there. You must help your child ask the questions that will expose that attitude of the heart that has resulted in wrong behavior." [11] Through disciplining and instructing your children, you are helping them understand the sinful motivations of their heart and their failure to trust God. You are leading them away from a destructive path and toward knowing, trusting, and obeying the perfect, heavenly Father.

DO IT NOW

Let me provide a few practical pointers on parenting.

- *Confess your sin.* Paul's words in Ephesians 6:4 and Colossians 3:21, about not provoking your children, are to you as a father. This means that you must admit where you have provoked your children, where you have failed to discipline them in love, and where you have neglected godly instruction. Before you remove the speck of your children's disobedience and rebellion, you must remove the plank of your failure to parent them according to God's design. Confess to your wife, to your community, and even to your children where you have sinned as a father. Ask a trusted friend to help point out your blind spots in parenting. Give him an open invitation to speak to you if he ever sees anything concerning.

- *Spend time with your children.* Perhaps no habit will so shape your relationship with your children as spending time with them. Find ways to spend one-on-one time with each of them, perhaps through special trips or breakfast dates or shared interests. Search for the appropriate mix of quality time and quantity time. The best opportunities for modeling the way of Christ, for encouraging them, and for raising them into maturity comes in the informal, everyday margin of life.

- *Enjoy your children.* There is little doubt that parenting has plenty of moments of exasperation and discouragement. As much as we love our children, we can grow weary of them and grow weary of the task of raising them. But we need to learn to find joy in them, even when they are at their most difficult. Instead of provoking them to anger, find ways to encourage them and celebrate them. A host of older parents will tearfully tell you just how quickly the years went past, how they regret their exasperation, and how they wish they could return to the days when their children were young.

- *Get parenting help.* There are many good books on parenting, and there is value in reading at least a couple of them (such as *Shepherding a Child's Heart* or *The Disciple-Making Parent*). But even better, find someone in your local church who has raised his children successfully, disciplining them in love and instructing them in godliness. Take that person out for coffee and say something like this: "I want my children to end up like your children. Tell me what you did." Listen humbly, consider carefully, and imitate wisely.

- *Parent with confidence.* If 21 years can bring us 75,000 new books on parenting, there must be 75 million blog articles and listicles. The sheer volume of counselors can confuse and discourage us. The opportunity for comparison that comes through social media can dishearten us. But if you are raising your children in the discipline and instruction of the Lord, if you are raising your children under the watchful eye of friends and pastors who have the freedom to speak into your life, you can parent boldly. Be confident that God is at work in your children through your efforts, however meager they may seem.

RUN TO WIN!

Few callings are as joy-filled and as sacred as the calling of father. Yet few callings are as difficult and leave you feeling so inadequate. Perhaps this is part of God's plan to cause you to rely on him all the more. You can trust that through the Bible and through the inner witness of the Holy Spirit, you have all you need to be the father God has called you to be. You can trust that he is willing to forgive your faults, to redeem your failures, and to glorify himself through your children. If you are going to run to win, you must nurture your children.

STRENGTH FOR THE RACE

Like the principles concerning marriage at the end of Ephesians 5, the ones about parenting at the beginning of chapter 6 can also be traced back grammatically to the command in Ephesians 5:18 to "be filled with the Spirit." And the similar parenting principles in Colossians 3:21 flow from the command to "let the word of Christ dwell in you richly" in verse 16. So the Spirit and the Word are our primary sources of strength (and comfort) as we attempt to achieve what seems like "Mission: Impossible"—loving and leading our children to genuine, lifelong relationships with Christ. As Jesus said, "With man this is impossible, but with God all things are possible" (Matthew 19:26). And it's also important to remember that God is still your loving Father even when you haven't been the best one to your children—that will help you to remain hopeful, and to bear with them through their own struggles and failures.

FINISH STRONG

I always read the biblical books of Kings and Chronicles with a sense of trepidation. I know these historical books fairly well, but every time I read of a new king taking the throne, I dread the inevitable assessment of his reign: Was he faithful or disobedient? Did he follow God or turn aside to false gods?

Asa was one of the good kings. He ruled Judah for 41 years and "did what was right in the eyes of the LORD, as David his father had done" (1 Kings 15:11). His rule was successful, his reign was honoring to God. He fought and won a great war against the Egyptians because he called out to God and had faith in his deliverance: "The LORD defeated the Ethiopians before Asa and before Judah, and the Ethiopians fled" (2 Chronicles 14:12). He enacted key religious reforms: "He took away the foreign altars and the high places and broke down the pillars and cut down the Asherim and commanded Judah to seek the LORD, the God of their fathers, and to keep the law and the commandment" (2 Chronicles 14:3–4). Perhaps most difficult of all, he removed his mother from her honorific position because of her stubborn idolatry. He was a good king to the end. Actually, not quite. He was a good king almost to the end.

In the 36th year of his reign, almost 90 percent of the way through, he had new trouble with Baasha, the king of Israel. This time, though, Asa did not rely on God but took matters into his own hands. Instead of crying out for deliverance as he had done before, he acted on his own, emptying the national treasury to bribe the Syrians to turn on Israel. Then, when he became ill, he neglected to seek God's help but instead relied entirely on physicians. For his lack of reliance upon God, he faced divine anger. Now, he was told, he would have constant warfare until the end of his reign and would also be struck with a crippling disease. Asa ruled well for so long and then collapsed. For 36 long years he was faithful; for five short years he was not.

As I ponder Asa, I consider the sorrow of finishing poorly and the joy of finishing well. I consider the terrible reality that a man can live a good life almost to the end, then falter, stumble, and even fall. This is why we so often hear of Christian leaders who had long and faithful ministries, who stood firm in the face of falsehood, who endured trials and persecution, but who then seemed to give way so much in their later years. We also hear of men who remained married to their wives for decades, then walked away near the end. What a tragedy. My friend, if you are going to run to win, you need to finish strong.

RUNNING AND FINISHING

A good long-distance runner knows the importance of planning his race. Even as he crosses the starting line he is already considering how he will cross the finish line. Even as he takes his first easy step, he has planned how he will take his last grueling step. A marathon runner may run 25 strong miles, but if he stops before his 26th, what good does that do him? Anyone can start a race, but only training and planning can prepare him to finish it. There are no prizes for almost crossing the finish line. In that sense, the final mile is the most important of all, the last steps are even more important than the first. A strong finish can make up for a weak start, but dropping out before the finish line negates even the most amazing early progress. Any imposter can start a race, but only a true athlete will finish it.

As a Christian man, you are already running the race of life, and I trust you are running in such a way that you will be victorious. Paul says, "Do you not know that in a race all the runners run, but only one receives the prize? So run that you may obtain it" (1 Corinthians 9:24). To obtain that prize, you will need to run to the very end. You will need to cross that finish line. And to do that, you will need to plan your race. You will need to plan the ways you will run today so you can continue to run in the difficult days ahead. Far better a weak start with a strong finish than a strong start followed by a complete collapse. No runner regrets finishing too strong, but many regret finishing too weak.

You are not competing against other people in this race

but against the deadly enemies of the world, the flesh, and the devil. How are you battling them? How do you plan to maintain your pace throughout the race? That is exactly what this entire book has been about. There is so much more that could be said, but I have outlined this plan according to disciplines related to faith, disciplines related to life, and disciplines related to relationship.

DISCIPLINES OF FAITH

- Embrace Your Purpose
- Renew Your Mind
- Know Your Doctrine
- Practice Your Devotion
- Prioritize Your Church
- Maintain Your Vigilance

DISCIPLINES OF LIFE

- Redeem Your Time
- Act Your Age
- Pursue Your Vocation
- Master Your Finances
- Guard Your Health
- Control Your Sexuality
- Consider Your Legacy

DISCIPLINES OF RELATIONSHIP

- Foster Your Friendships
- Accept Your Leadership
- Treasure Your Marriage
- Nurture Your Children

I am convinced that if you pursue these disciplines, you will be pacing yourself well and preparing yourself to cross the finish line with arms raised in victory. You will be setting the pace to finish the race. You, like Paul, will be able to say with confidence, "I have fought the good fight, I have finished the race, I have kept the faith. Henceforth there is laid up for me the crown of righteousness, which the Lord, the righteous judge, will award to me on that day, and not only to me but also to all who have loved his appearing" (2 Timothy 4:7–8).

I will give the final word to J.I. Packer who, in the final steps of his race, has written these words: "Runners in a distance race… always try to keep something in reserve for a final sprint. And my contention is that, so far as our bodily health allows, we should aim to be found running the last lap of the race of our Christian life, as we would say, flat out. The final sprint, so I urge, should be a sprint indeed."[12]

If you are going to run to win, you must finish strong.

ENDNOTES

1. Donald Whitney, *Spiritual Disciplines for the Christian Life* (NavPress, 2014), p 167.

2. Timothy Keller, *Every Good Endeavor* (Penguin Books, 2012), p 181.

3. Jerry Bridges, *The Pursuit of Holiness* (NavPress, 2006), p 87.

4. J.R. Miller, *Home-Making* (Presbyterian Board of Publication, 1882), p 277.

5. Hugh Black, *Friendship* (London: Hodder & Stoughton, 1897), p 90.

6. These four headings are adapted from Richard Phillips, *Ephesians: A Mentor Expository Commentary* (Scotland: Christian Focus Publications, 2016), pp 409-415.

7. Ibid, p 413

8. https://twitter.com/drsferguson/status/639047612386119680

9. Chap Bettis, *The Disciple-Making Parent* (Diamond Hill Publishing, 2016), p 6.

10. Tedd Tripp, *Shepherding a Child's Heart* (United States of America: Shepherd Press, 1995), p 107.

11. Ibid, p 5.

12. J. I. Packer, *Finishing Our Course with Joy* (Crossway, 2014), p 21.

Do More Better
A Practical Guide to Productivity

Tim Challies | 114 pages

Don't try to do it all. Do more good. Better.

bit.ly/domorebetter

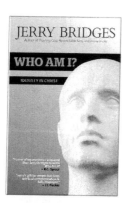

Who Am I?
Identity in Christ

Jerry Bridges | 91 pages

Jerry Bridges unpacks Scripture to give the Christian eight clear, simple, interlocking answers to one of the most essential questions of life.

bit.ly/WHOAMI

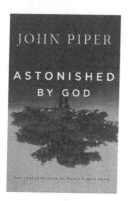

Astonished by God
Ten Truths to Turn the World Upside Down

John Piper | 192 pages

Turn your world on its head.

bit.ly/AstonishedbyGod

Two books by Peter Krol

Knowable Word
*Helping Ordinary People
Learn to Study the Bible
(Revised and Expanded)*
bit.ly/Knowable

Sowable Word
*Helping Ordinary People
Learn to Lead Bible
Studies*
bit.ly/Sowable

The Company We Keep
In Search of Biblical Friendship

Jonathan Holmes
Foreword by Ed Welch | 112 pages

*Biblical friendship is deep, honest, pure,
tranparent, and liberating. It is also attainable.*

bit.ly/B-Friend

The God of the Mundane:
Reflections on Ordinary Life
for Ordinary People

(second edition)

Matthew B. Redmond | 134 pages

*It's OK to not be a "radical" Christian. Our life is
not about what we do for God. It's about what he
does for us.*

bit.ly/MUNDANE

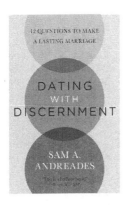

Dating with Discernment: 12 Questions to Make a Lasting Marriage

Sam A. Andreades | 280 pages

A fresh, biblical paradigm for choosing a spouse.

"This is a brilliant book!" – Rosaria Butterfield
"Profoundly insightful" – Joel R. Beeke

bit.ly/DatingWell

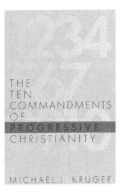

The Ten Commandments of Progressive Christianity

Michael J. Kruger | 56 pages

A cautionary look at ten dangerously appealing half-truths.

bit.ly/TENCOM

Endorsed by Collin Hansen,
Kevin DeYoung, Michael Horton

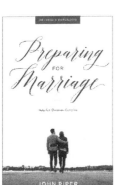

Preparing for Marriage
Help for Christian Couples

John Piper | 86 pages

As you prepare for marriage, dare to dream with God.

bit.ly/prep-for-marriage

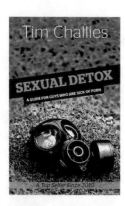

Sexual Detox
A Guide for Guys Who Are Sick of Porn

by Tim Challies | 90 pages

Reorient your understanding of sex, according to God's plan for this great gift

bit.ly/SEXUALDETOX

Getting Back in the Race
The Cure for Backsliding

Joel R. Beeke | 103 pages

Learn the diagnosis. experience the cure.

bit.ly/THERACE

Servanthood as Worship
The Privilege of Life in a Local Church

Nate Palmer | 112 pages

Celebrating our calling to serve in the church, motivated by the grace that is ours in the gospel.

bit.ly/Srvnt